PLAYING WITH BOOKS

THE ART OF UPCYCLING, DECONSTRUCTING, & REIMAGINING THE BOOK

Jason Thompson

BEVERLY, MASSACHUSETTS

QUARRY

CONTENTS

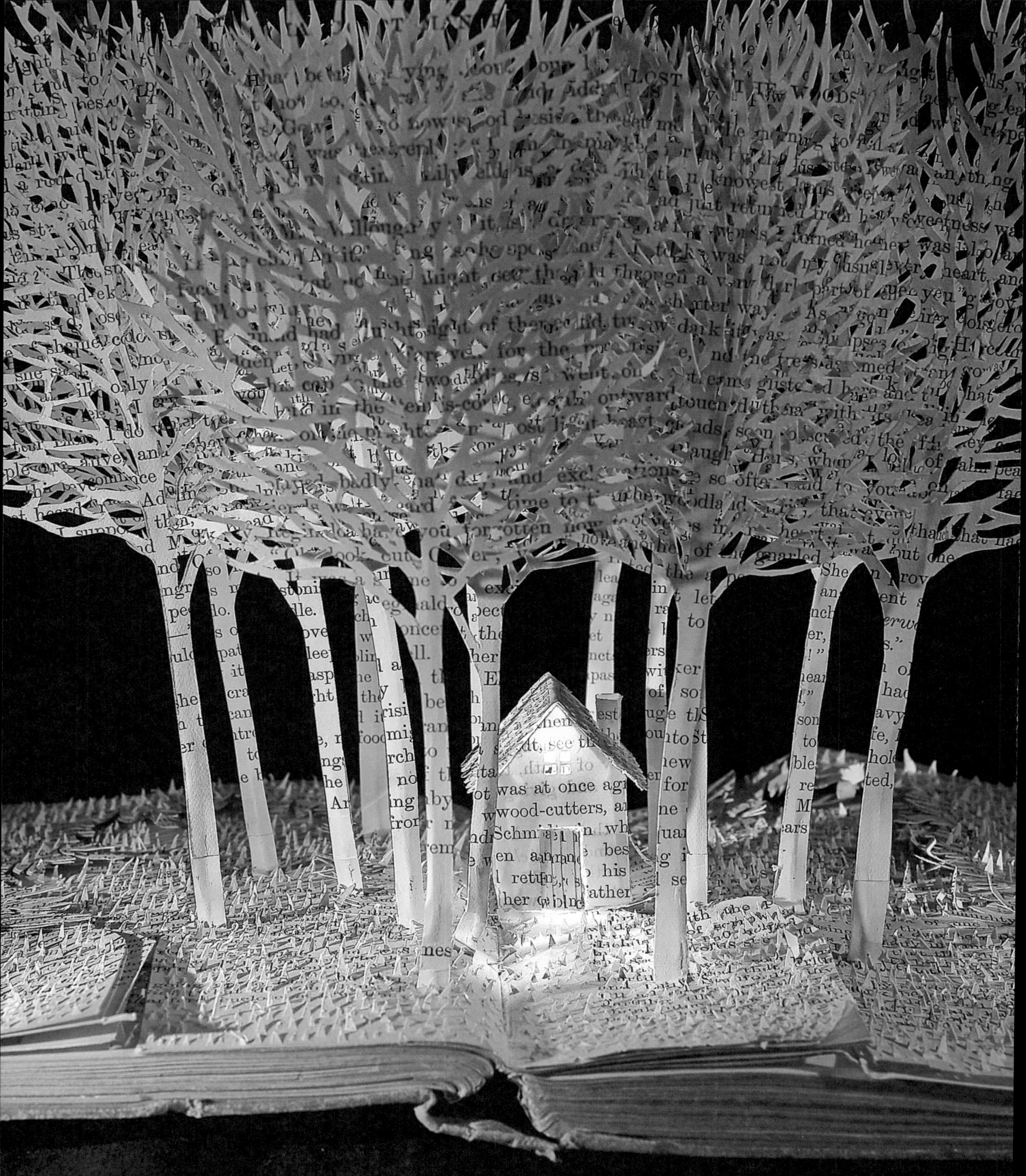

Books are more than pages, board, glue, and thread—they are artifacts of the human spirit and hand.

Who among us doesn't love books? My lifelong interest began as a small child listening attentively to my mother reading bedtime stories by Dr. Seuss, Margaret Wise Brown, and Maurice Sendak. Books have been a part of my personal and professional life ever since: As a bookbinder, I'm surrounded by them and consider myself better educated and more creative because of my love for books and bookish things.

I discovered bookbinding quite by accident. Twenty years ago, I met a Rhode Island School of Design graduate who learned bookbinding firsthand while apprenticing in Assisi, Italy, in a small shop just off the main Piazza. She studied fine binding and constructed small blank journals to sell to tourists who happened upon the picturesque studio. On her return to New England, she taught me the craft, and I fell in love with the process—and with her. Those initial bookbinding experiments, carried out in our small Providence, Rhode Island, apartment, are the only lessons I've taken as a bookbinder, yet I've run a successful bindery for twenty years. I acquired my bookbinding skills through practice and curiosity. I share this to inspire anyone who has a dream but feels a lack of education is a barrier to success. If I—a high school drop out—can do it, so can you.

I consider books to be precious, and, more than I like to admit, I often appreciate them as beautiful objects, regardless of their content. In my office, I display a collection of books by the nineteenth-century polar explorer Fridtjof Nansen. When my daughter was six, she once asked how many of them I had read and was perplexed when I told her I had only read three. The answer, though truthful, was odd to me, too: several well-tended shelves of Nansen books, but I had only read three.

Books are meant to be read, of course, but for some of us who appreciate books for more than their printed content they exert a charm. They are objects to fetishize. This preciousness is what drives book collectors to acquire books they might never read. Favorite, well-read books, carefully organized bookshelves, the smell of a used-book store, endless aisles of library stacks: these are the components of the book-lover's world. But to fully understand the industry of publishing and bookmaking, we have to consider, too, the lowly computer manual—indispensable one moment, in the garbage the next—as well as the myriad textbooks, self-help guides, recipe collections, political tomes, and contemporary novels, once timely, then forgotten. The publishing industry produced more than 3 billion books in 2008. With so many books competing for space annually on bookstore shelves, those that aren't bestsellers, or even adequate sellers, are moved aside for new titles. The result of this overabundance of books is that many wind up in remainder bins and then eventually, if we're honest, into the recycling bin and landfill.

Is there a purpose for some of these unwanted books? Answering this question leads us to artists, designers, and artisans who appreciate books in a uniquely different way. Although the fundamental parts of a book might consist of pages and covers, the artist's eye sees something more: raw materials to create unique objects far removed from the book form. To these artists, books are resources to rearrange, recycle, and reimagine into functional and decorative objects.

I was hesitant the first time I ripped a book apart to extract its paper pages for a bookish project. It felt wrong to cannibalize the essence of a book for its elemental parts. But after playing with enough unwanted and forgotten books, this feeling eventually passed. There are a lot of books out there—don't be afraid to exorcise their bookish essence for other creative ends.

The following pages feature work from artists who turn the book form on its head by using bookbinding, woodworking, paper crafting, origami, textile, and decorative arts techniques. They follow the process from pulp to paper to printing and binding and then beyond for an array of creative mutilations and dissections.

We cannot hope to save all the books from the landfill—this is a Sisyphean task. But we can be inspired by the creativity of these artists, who reinterpret both lowly and lofty books into something more.

I eventually married my bookbinding instructor; together, we run our family bindery and enjoy watching our young daughter play with old books, paper, and glue. The journey of book appreciation has certainly come full circle when we can, without reserve, both save our precious and important books and tear apart the unwanted ones.

—JASON THOMPSON

Su Blackwell, *The Woodcutter's Hut*/2008
Courtesy Su Blackwell and Long & Ryle Gallery

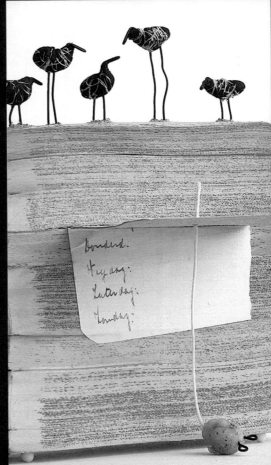

FOLD, MUTILATE, STAPLE & SPINDLE

CHAPTER }

Before you jump in and start tearing apart books for art projects, take a moment to consider the materials you'll need. Here are a few basic descriptions of adhesives, cutting materials, and other bookbinding and paper-crafting tools, as well as a diagram showing the basic parts of a book.

ADHESIVES

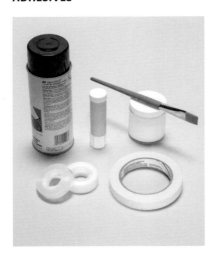

PVA Glue

The first glue I always reach for is water-based PVA (polyvinyl acetate) white glue. It's available at most art stores and online in many sizes, from pint-sized (473 ml) containers to 5-gallon (19 liter) buckets. PVA is applicable to most paper and bookbinding projects. It dries clear and is archival and easy to work with. It can be mixed with water to extend its drying time and easily washes off brushes.

General Purpose White Glue

An alternative to PVA is white glue. It's non-archival and can be crunchy and inflexible when dry, so avoid using this glue for projects that are meant to be saved, need to be flexible, or in which strong adhesion is necessary. That said, you can find white glue just about everywhere. Don't be afraid to use it on temporary projects or for kids' crafts.

Spray Mount

Spray mount is used as an alternative to other adhesives for projects in this book for two applications: to adhere materials that would otherwise warp with water-based glues and to laminate paper to clear plastic. You can create a faux fabric material (think reusable shopping bags) by laminating paper to clear plastic and sewing it as you would fabric. Spray mount tends to get everywhere, so, whenever possible, use it outdoors.

Glue Sticks

Applicator sticks of glue are convenient, and some brands claim to be archival. However, glue sticks can be unreliable for adhesive-intensive projects and can dry out over time. Use glue sticks for kids' projects and temporary creations.

Transparent Tape

This kind of tape, commonly used for wrapping gifts, is convenient for non-archival, temporary applications. Major brands adhere to paper well and can be used for many paper crafting projects, especially by kids. If archival properties are important, use PVA instead.

Artist Tape

This multipurpose tape is repositionable, doesn't leave residue when it's removed, and eventually dries to a permanent fix. It is similar to masking tape but is much easier to work with. Use artist tape to hinge board or to temporarily hold materials together while you work.

Double-sided Tape

This tape is acid-free and easy to use directly from the roll. Use double-sided tape to laminate materials together, but use care when adhering materials that are under stress—paper rolls and rolled beads, for example, might not remain securely fastened when taped. The paper, which wants to return to its unrolled state, will eventually unroll.

CUTTING TOOLS

Scissors

The most reliable scissors I use for paper crafting and bookbinding are an 8" (20 cm) pair from Fiskars that are laminated with a nonstick coating, which is helpful when cutting through paper pages that have been laminated or adhered with sticky adhesive. When buying a pair of scissors, spend a little extra; good ones last longer and keep a sharp cutting edge. If you buy good scissors, consider buying scissor sharpeners. A good pair of scissors will benefit from sharpening, whereas cheap scissors generally suffer from other issues in addition to a dull cutting edge: they often become loose when they get old, for example, at which point sharpening doesn't help.

Knives and Mats

Use a cutting knife or utility blade to take apart books or slice through stacks of paper. Replace dull blades as often as possible. You're more likely to injure yourself when using a dull blade than when using a sharp one because of the extra force and pressure needed to cut through materials. Using a cutting mat protects your work surface and allows you to easily make straight and perpendicular cuts.

PUNCHES AND CIRCLE CUTTERS
Circular Hole Punches

When I first started bookbinding and paper crafting, only one type of circular hole punch was available: the metal ¼" (6 mm) punches found at office supply stores, which were anything but comfortable. Fortunately, punches are now available in a variety of hole sizes and are ergonomically designed with soft handles. Punches are handy for paper jewelry projects and making ornaments.

Circle Cutters and Circular Dies

Probably the most fun of all paper-crafting tools—for kids and adults alike—are circle cutters. These are available in two basic designs: dies or rotating blade holders. Circular die punches are handheld and create one fixed size per punch. These are quick and easy to use and are fun for kids. Rotating blade holders can be used to cut a variety of circle sizes; however, they require a steady hand and a solid work surface. Replace blades often and always use a cutting mat.

LAMINATING

Hand Laminating

This specialized technique creates a laminated paper-and-plastic material that can be worked like fabric. Spray mount adhesive is used to adhere the materials together, and the clear plastic is the same stuff our grandparents used to slip-cover upholstery. It can be purchased by the roll at fabric shops or online and is available in different thicknesses (also referred to as gauges or mil weights); thinner is better for this application.

To laminate plastic to paper, coat a piece of paper with spray mount and adhere it to the clear plastic material. Repeat the process with the other side of the paper to complete the lamination process (the paper should be sandwiched between two sheets of plastic). The resulting paper-and-plastic laminate can be used like a textile to create bags, hats, aprons, and more. Cut it with scissors and sew it by hand or with a sewing machine.

LAMINATING (CONTINUED...)

Machine Laminating

Laminating machines place a thin coating of adhesive to the back of just about any type of flat material, from cardboard to tissue paper. The adhesive is acid-free and very strong. To use, place the material into the feeding tray and turn the handle. The machine applies a thin layer of permanent or temporary adhesive to the materials and then sends it to the cutting tray. Laminating machines and adhesive refills are available at craft stores and online. (I often use the ones manufactured by Xyron.) Use laminating machines in place of spray or wet adhesive to quickly wrap boards on temporary projects.

CUTTING AND SHAPING BOOKS

Shaping Books by Hand

In this technique, the fore-edge of a book is shaped with a craft knife, leaving the spine intact, and fanned open 360 degrees to create a three-dimensional object. The simplest way to shape a book is to cut it by hand. Begin by removing the covers, then clamp a thin wood or cardboard template to the book. With a sharp blade, slice the pages, using the edge of the template as a guide. The final piece often has a hand-cut look to the edges.

Shaping Books with a Tabletop Jig Saw

To shape a book with a tabletop jig saw, secure a book between two pieces of wood (roughly the same size as the book) by

screwing or bolting the boards and book together, like a book sandwich. Using a tabletop jig saw, cut through both the book and boards to create the desired shape. The screw or bolt holes are generally not seen when the book is fanned open, unless they fall near the outer edge of the book. The disadvantage to this technique is that it can be difficult to cut two different books in exactly the same pattern if two books are required to create one project, such as a vase, for example. Note that the wood is not reused.

Shaping Books with a Router

Using a router requires a template. Although the templates I use are custom laser cut (and I suspect most readers won't go through the effort to have templates laser cut), a template cut from ³⁄₈" (1 cm) MDF board or plywood with a jig saw works just as well. Two identical templates are required, so cut both at the same time. Place the book between the templates and hand tighten with bolts and wing nuts. Using a bearing-guided straight bit, cut and shape the book by following the edge of the template. The benefits to this technique are that every time a book is cut, it is the exact same shape, and the templates can be used over and over again.

PAPIER MÂCHÉ AND DECOUPAGE

Papier Mâché

In this technique, strips of paper are soaked in an adhesive medium such as wheat paste or diluted white glue and used to cover an armature, creating a firm, hollow object. Small decorative objects created entirely from book pages can be constructed with this technique. Papier mâché objects are usually painted, the paper used only as a structural element, but when book pages are used, the paper itself forms the decorative surface.

Decoupage

Similar to papier mâché, decoupage uses paper, such as book pages, to completely cover objects, including furniture, containers, and decorative items. Use white glue, acrylic medium, or decoupage mediums to adhere the paper and collage in decorative or random patterns. Polyurethane can be used to seal the decoupage.

FOLDING BOOKS

Folding Book Pages

Folding is a fun and easy way to turn a book into a three-dimensional object, and it's kid-friendly. You can remove the book covers, especially from paperbacks, before folding—this makes the folding easier and the final folded book more attractive—but leaving the covers on a hardcover book provides a structural "stand" to hold the folded book in position for display.

Straight Folding

Remove the front and back covers from a paperback book and fold every page in half toward the gutter and spine. Depending on the number of pages, the thickness of the paper, and the grain direction, when completed, the book will be transformed into a half-cylinder shape. Folding two same-sized books in this manner and placing them back to back creates a standing cylinder. Use paperclips, bobby pins, or adhesive to attach two half-cylinder books together.

Angle and Pattern Folding

Fold pages at an angle by turning one corner in toward the gutter and spine. The folks at my favorite used-book store folded a number of books this way. The books ranged from very large to very small and were stacked one on top of another, like a holiday tree. Experiment with alternating folds: one page to the right, the next to the left. Or try cutting the pages to create multiple folds per page. Or fold the pages in a progressive pattern, each successive page at a slightly different angle. Experiment and have fun.

ROLLING AND BEADING

Paper-rolling Tools

Use a wooden skewer, paintbrush handle, chopstick, pencil, or thin metal rod as a rolling tool to create paper beads, rolls, and tubes of paper. For fine rolling, such as creating beads for jewelry, use a needle, thin wire, or a paper bead–winding tool designed specifically for creating paper beads.

Paper Tubes

To create a long, thin tube, begin with a square piece of paper and roll the sheet from edge to edge around your rolling tool. Note that paper pages often have a grain direction, which can be noticeable when rolling—rolling from top to bottom might be easier than rolling from side to side, for example; practice both ways before creating tubes. Before completing the roll, apply adhesive to the edge of the paper, finish rolling, and then hold the tube together for a moment while the adhesive sets. White glue applied with a brush works best.

Paper Rolls

This technique creates a roll that is thicker at the center than at the edges and takes advantage of the printed design of the paper used to create the roll. The design of the printed paper used for the roll will fall randomly along the length of the roll creating an unexpected pattern. Begin with a square sheet of paper and roll from corner to corner. Grain direction won't be much of an issue with this technique. However, application of the adhesive is important, because the glued area is just a small corner, not the full length of the sheet, so use adhesive liberally.

Paper Beads

Create paper beads by using a very long, tapered triangular piece of paper—for example, 10" (25.4 cm) long and 2" (5.1 cm) wide at one end and tapering to a point at the other end. Begin by rolling the 2" (5.1 cm) end and continue rolling until the point is almost reached. Stop rolling with 1.5" (3.8 cm) of the point to go and liberally apply white glue along the point. Finish rolling the bead. The adhesive will extrude and smear, but this is okay. Continue spinning the completed bead, using your fingers to coat the entire outside of the bead with white glue. This final step prevents the bead from unrolling. Paper beads can also be coated with a clear polyurethane.

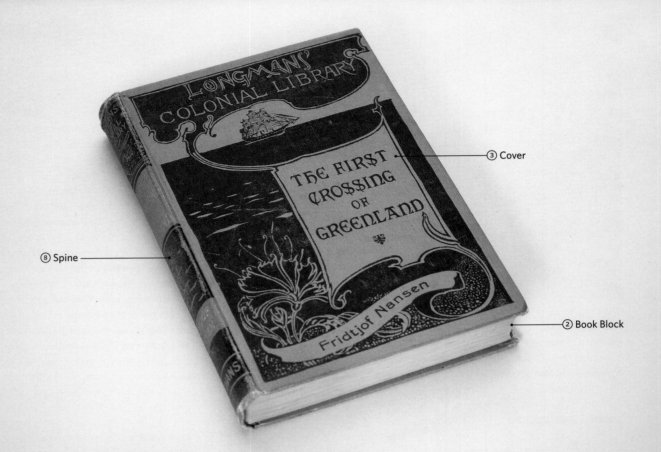

③ Cover

⑧ Spine

② Book Block

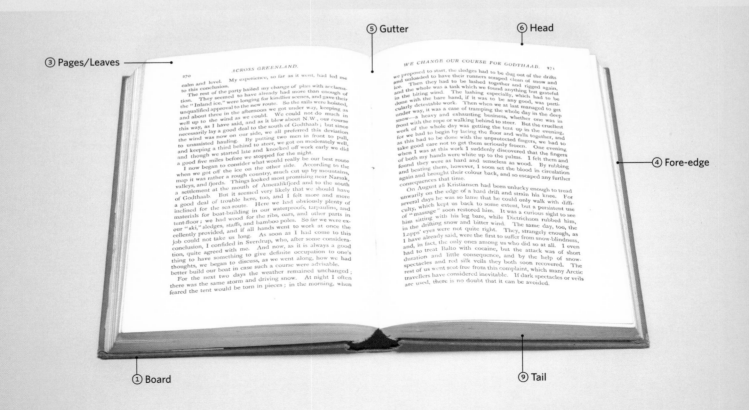

⑤ Gutter

⑥ Head

③ Pages/Leaves

④ Fore-edge

① Board

⑨ Tail

ANATOMY OF A BOOK

These basic definitions cover the general terms used for the projects in this book. Books on bookbinding often define the parts of a book in more detail.

① **Board:** the material that provides rigidity to the covers of hardcover books; it is usually covered with cloth, leather, or paper.

② **Book Block:** a block of pages, created when book pages are sewn or glued together before being bound into the book covers; also, the pages of a book that remain after the book covers have been removed.

③ **Cover:** on a hardcover, the outer casing, usually made from board, that wraps around the text block and protects the pages; on a paperback, the heavy paper wrapping that covers the book block.

④ **Fore-edge:** The "front" or unbound edge of the book's pages that sit opposite the spine.

⑤ **Gutter:** the crease or fold in the center of a book when it is open, created when the book pages are sewn or glued together; the area where the left-hand and right-hand pages meet.

⑥ **Head:** the top edge of the book when it is standing upright; includes the cover, spine, and book block.

⑦ **Pages/Leaves:** The printed and bound paper pages, usually folded into signatures (collections of folded sheets) and sewn and/or glued together to form a book block.

⑧ **Spine:** The part of the book that covers the glue, mull (the open-weave fabric that lines the spine), and sewn side of the book block; it's the part that's seen when the book is placed on a bookshelf.

⑨ **Tail:** The bottom edge of the book on which it rests when standing upright; includes the cover, spine, and book block.

- **What's a Book?** Types of books you can repurpose for the projects featured in this book include old books, children's books, foreign-language books, sheet music collections, comic books, phone books, books of ornithology, lepidoptery, and other natural collections, ledgers, handwritten books, journals and diaries, poetry collections, art books, school books, catalogues, crossword puzzle collections, zines, romance novels, classic fiction, science fiction, pulp fiction, and just about any type of bound volume that can be taken apart for its raw materials.

- **Where to Find Books:** To take books apart, they need to be handy, but your living room bookcase isn't always the right place to look for unwanted books. We all own a book or two we can live without, but boxes of books in different sizes, on different topics, and with a variety of bindings are a resource much like a paint box is to a painter. Boxes of unwanted books are easier to find than you might think.

- **The Library:** I contacted the fundraising group for our local library branch and asked if the library had books left over from its annual book sales. I was invited to the library and was led to a basement room with literally thousands of books piled in tumbling towers of boxes and told to help myself. Libraries are continually acquiring new books, but they're disposing of them regularly, too.

- **Classifieds:** Enter "Free Books" into the FOR SALE section of any of the numerous online classified-ad websites and you'll be amazed at the number of listings you can find on any given day.

- **Used-book Stores:** The storage rooms of most used-book stores are filled with books that won't sell. One of the booksellers in my hometown had several boxes in a back room and was more than happy to give them away. Another has a permanent "FREE" sign in the doorway on a box regularly overflowing with unwanted books.

- **The Dump:** Check the municipal dump in your town—it might have an area set aside for visitors to drop off items for others to salvage. A dump a few towns away from us has even set aside a "bookshelf" specifically for books.

- **The Side of the Road:** This might not be the first place to look for books, but once the idea of recycling books into art is planted in your psyche, you'll find that the odd box of books can show up anywhere, including the side of the road, frequently after a yard sale.

PROJECTS TO PLAY WITH:
NOVEL IDEAS FOR ARTISTS & BIBLIOPHILES

CHAPTER

}

Discarded

}

OLD BOOKS WITH ENGRAVINGS AND ETCHINGS can be salvaged for their illustrations. Use collage techniques to create one-of-a-kind cards suitable for birthdays, holidays, thank you, even wedding and birth announcements.

DESIGN A ONE-OF-A-KIND CARD

Resources for collage elements can be found in many types of discarded books, including children's books, comic books, history and travel books, coffee-table books, photography collections, and books about birds, butterflies, animals, and other flora and fauna. For the card base, use watercolor paper folded in half. Apply elements cut from book pages with white glue and a glue brush. The birdman card was designed using materials from two books: one containing Victorian portraits and another about North American birds.

✴ TIPS:

Photocopies of illustrated elements can be used to create multiple copies of the same card. Photocopy the individual designs and collage each element one at a time to retain a handmade look and feel. Color black-and-white elements to make each card unique.

✄ MATERIALS

discarded illustrated books
scissors
white glue
glue brush
watercolor paper

💬 CONSIDERATIONS

The design possibilities are end-less for this project. Recipients are sure to display these special, one-of-a-kind cards created just for them.

One-of-a-kind card created with collaged elements from old books

Artist: Kristin Sollenberger

Pier Gustafson
1 Fitchburg St.
B352
Somerville, Mass.
02143

Letters Home

ALMOST EVERY TYPE OF ENVELOPE is made from a single piece of paper folded and glued to create a pocket for letters. Custom envelopes are a snap to create and will impress your literary friends.

CREATING CUSTOM ENVELOPES

Designing a one-of-a-kind envelope is as simple as tracing the outline of a commercially manufactured envelope onto a decorative book page. Choose an envelope of the appropriate size and open the flaps on all four sides. Release the adhesive on the flaps by holding the envelope over steam, if necessary. Trace and cut out the envelope, then fold it to match the original envelope. Glue the flaps closed with white glue and a brush. TIP: Trace the outline of the envelope template lightly with a pencil, so it doesn't show on the inside or outside of the finished envelope.

✹ **TIP:**
Use cardboard to create permanent envelope templates of different shapes and sizes. Keep a stack handy to use whenever a custom envelope is needed.

✂ **MATERIALS**
book pages
scissors
pencil
white glue
glue brush
manufactured envelopes to use as templates

💬 **CONSIDERATIONS**
If the typography of the book pages makes reading a handwritten name and address on the envelope difficult, choose pages with words on one side only and fold them so the type falls on the inside of the envelope, or adhere a plain rectangle over the printed envelope to use as an address label.

Close-up of a book page envelope sealed with sealing wax

Artist: Jason Thompson

MOON ZERO

5 TA
TOMO

POST CARD
PLAYING WITH BOOKS

Wish you were here!

A breathtaki
journey throu
and space wit
top writers
of science fiction

GION
CE
MSON

enture from here to infinity . . .
arre of today to the
morrow.

Paperback Writer

OLD PAPERBACK BOOKS CAN BE FOUND just about everywhere and are sometimes even less expensive than commercially printed postcards. Many have interesting and unusual cover designs that can be turned into postcards.

DESIGN A ONE-OF-A-KIND POSTCARD

Most paperback covers will tear away easily from the book pages. Covers that are old or firmly adhered might require the use of a craft or utility knife. Once the cover is removed, clean away any glue residue. Use a corner cutter to create clean, rounded corners. The printed side of these science fiction postcards was designed on a computer and printed using a desktop printer. TIP: Be clever and choose a paperback title appropriate to the location and circumstances from where it will be sent.

✸ TIP:

Follow postal regulations when mailing paperback postcards—they might require additional postage or hand stamping by a postal worker to enter the postal system.

Paperback covers turned into postcards

Artist: Jason Thompson

✂ MATERIALS
paperback book covers
corner cutter
craft or utility knife (optional)

☞ CONSIDERATIONS
The idea for this project comes from a set of postcards I sent to a Swedish friend more than a decade ago. I mailed him a handmade postcard made from the paperback cover torn from a copy of Ian Fleming's *Moonraker*. He mailed back a postcard right away written on the back of Ian Fleming's *Thunderball*. And a tradition was created.

Pocketbook

SHOW OFF YOUR BOOKISH AFFECTIONS with a one-of-a-kind pocketbook made by lining the covers of a hardcover book with decorative fabric. Use favorite fabrics and embellish it with elements such as a designer tag and custom handles.

Artist: Ilira Steinman

✂ MATERIALS
decorative book covers
fabric
fabric shears
chipboard
spray mount
fabric glue
purse handles
utility blade

🗩 CONSIDERATIONS
Turn a hardcover book into a pocketbook. Any hardcover book will do—choose one by its color, design, or title. Use favorite decorator fabrics and repurpose old purse handles.

INSTRUCTIONS:

① **STEP ONE: GATHER THE MATERIALS**

Use a utility blade to carefully remove the outer covers and spine from a hardcover book. Be sure the spine remains intact and remove any bits of adhesive or paper from the inside of the covers. Cut two pieces of chipboard the same size as the book covers. Cut another piece of chipboard the same size as the spine.

② **STEP TWO: CREATE THE FABRIC PATTERN**

Each repurposed book requires its own custom fabric pattern. The dimensions of the fabric for the front and back panels should match the dimensions of the book covers. The measurements of the fabric for the purse

bottom should match the dimensions of the book spine. The fabric side panels are created by carefully measuring the "head" and "tail" of the book when it is opened to approximately 45 degrees. Create pairs of each of these five patterns—front, back, bottom, left-side, and right-side fabric panels—and sew each set of five fabric pieces into a purse shape, wrong sides together, facing the inside, as shown in figure 2.

③ **STEP THREE: CREATE THE STRUCTURE**

This step creates the rigid structure that is placed inside the fabric purse sewn together in the previous step. Wrap the three cardboard pieces created in Step One with decorative fabric. Position the cardboard pieces to mimic the shape of the book covers and use spray mount or a dry adhesive to attach the fabric. Wrap the fabric completely around one side and the edges of the cardboard pieces. It is not necessary to cover the backs, because they will be glued to the book cover and will not be seen in the finished pocketbook.

④ **STEP FOUR: ASSEMBLY**
Insert the fabric-covered cardboard pieces, right side facing up, into the fabric purse and adhere together with fabric glue. Attach the purse handles to the book covers according to the manufacturer's instructions, or, if the handles have been recycled, using appropriate steps so that they will be tightly attached to the book covers. Finally, place the entire purse assembly inside the book covers and attach it with a liberal amount of fabric glue. Embellish the purse with elements such as buttons or a designer tag.

✱ **TIPS:**
Add a zipper or flaps to the purse by adjusting the fabric pattern. Use a quilt-weight fabric; upholstery-weight fabrics can be too stiff for this application. Purse handles are available from craft stores or can be recycled from an unused purse. Fabric glue is available at fabric stores and online.

Pocketbook created using a vintage book

PROJECT NO. 5}
PAGE 28

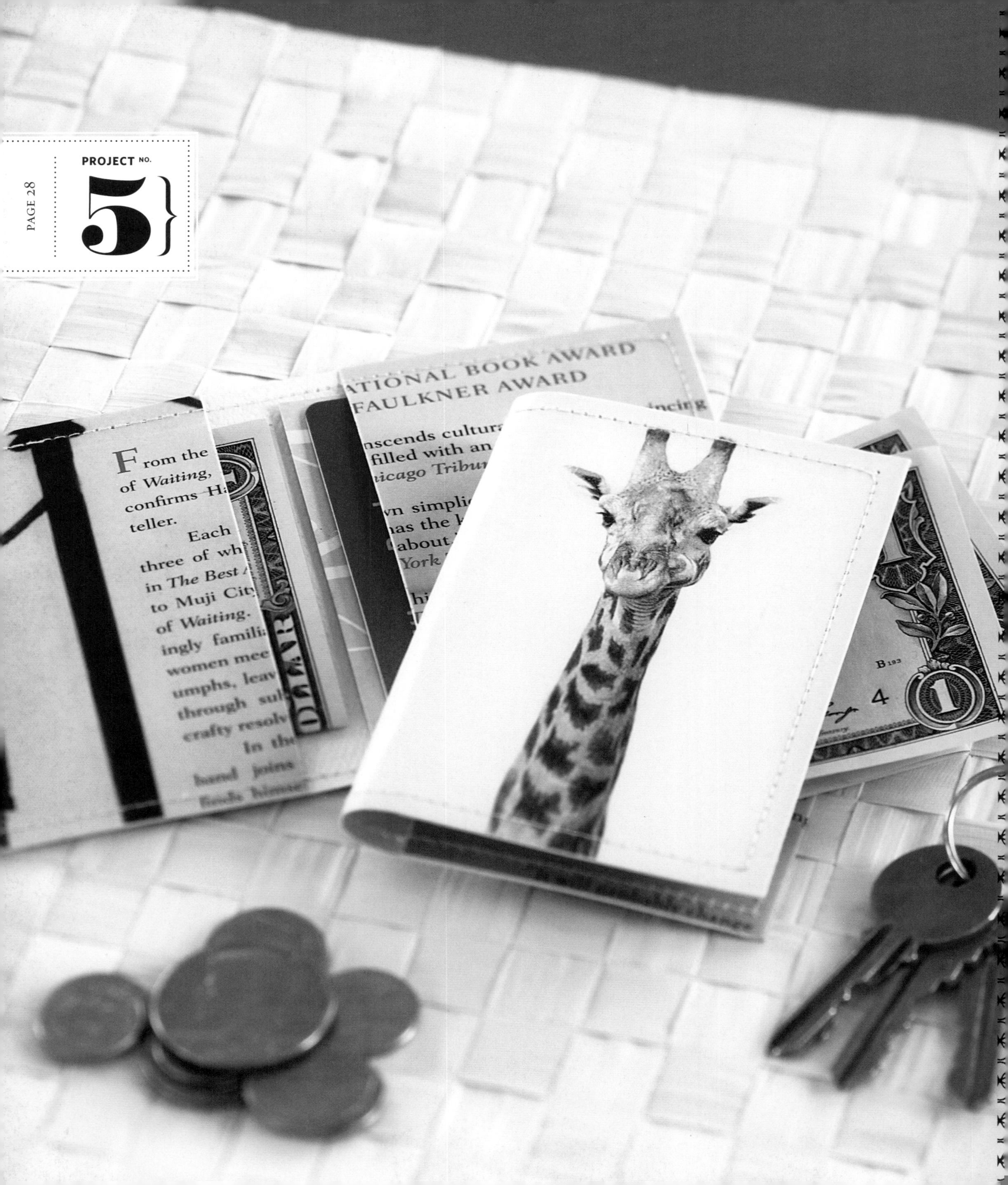

Artist: Jason Thompson

✂ MATERIALS
book jacket
cardstock
spray mount
scissors
sewing machine

💬 CONSIDERATIONS
Many modern book jackets are laminated with a waxy coating and can be spotted by their glossy look and smooth, waxy feel. These types of book jackets are appropriate for billfolds because they wear better than matte paper, the waxy coating serving as a barrier to dirt and moisture.

PROJECT 5: BOOK JACKET BILLFOLD

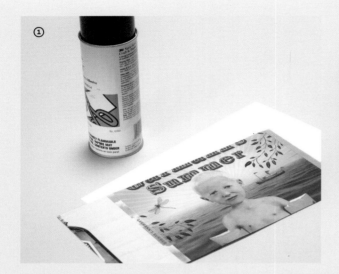

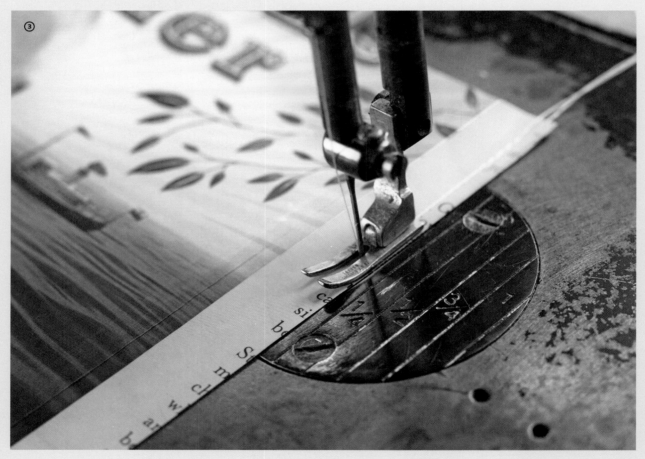

INSTRUCTIONS:

① STEP ONE:
ASSEMBLE THE MATERIALS

Trim the book jacket to 5" × 12" (12.7 × 30.5 cm). Most book jacket covers are shorter than 12" (30.5 cm) wide, so you will need to use the spine, back cover, and flaps to complete the 12" (30.5 cm) length. Cut a piece of flexible cardstock or heavyweight paper to the same dimensions. This material will line the inside of the billfold.

② STEP TWO: LAMINATE AND FOLD

Using spray mount, firmly laminate the book jacket and cardstock together. Allow to dry, then trim to 4" × 11" (10.2 × 27.9 cm). Fold both sides of the laminated cover inward 2.5" (6.5 cm) to form two pockets.

③ STEP THREE: SEW

Seal the edges of the billfold by machine-stitching around the outside edge of the entire billfold with a complementary color of thread.

✳ TIPS:

Place a temporary guide next to the presser foot on the sewing machine to create an even stitch around the perimeter of the billfold. For example, tape a metal ruler to the sewing machine bed parallel to the sewing foot as a guide along which to run the billfold. Additionally, insert credit cards into the billfold before sewing. Once sewn, the pockets will yawn open to accept additional cards or bills.

Close-up of stitching

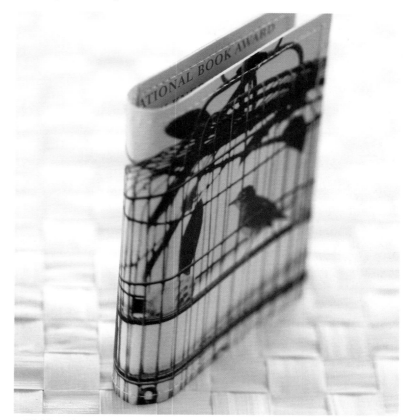

Billfold made using the book jacket from a hardcover book

Little Paper Houses

PROJECTS TO PLAY WITH

THESE LITTLE PAPER HOUSES are made using book pages folded into squares and triangles. Display paper houses as decorative objects, or present them as a housewarming gift.

Artist: Jason Thompson

✂ **MATERIALS**
book pages
scissors

⬤ CONSIDERATIONS
This project is adapted from an origami technique used to create business card cubes. The folds are simple enough for children to attempt. The base, sides, and peaked roof are created using just one type of fold, which creates the different "flaps," "slots," and "panels" necessary to assemble the basic house. A second fold creates the triangular "gable" attached to the roof.

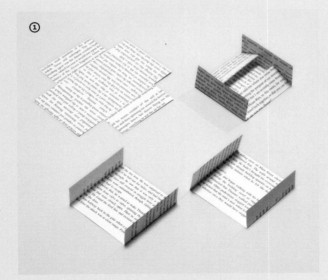

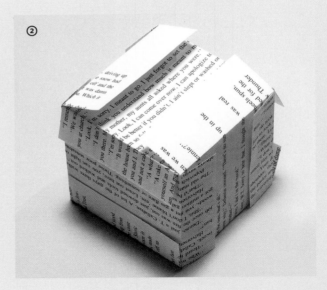

Detail

✺ TIP:
Construct an entire paper village: Place the houses over strings of holiday lights to create a group of paper houses that glow from within.

INSTRUCTIONS:

① **STEP ONE: BASIC FOLD**
Cut twenty-one book pages to 2.5" × 4" (6.4 × 10.2 cm). Working with two pieces at a time, place one on top of the other at right angles. Fold both flaps of the bottom piece upward to create a square panel. Repeat with the other piece. Separate the two pieces to create folded book pages, each with two flaps and a perfectly centered, square panel. Fold sixteen of these basic shapes and leave the remaining five pieces unfolded.

② **STEP TWO: ASSEMBLE THE BASE**
Place six pieces together to form a cube (figure 2 and figure 2 detail). When assembled correctly, the flaps of each piece will hug the adjoining panel. No adhesive is necessary to create this cube; however, the cube will be flimsy until the next step is completed.

③ **STEP THREE: STABILIZE THE BASE**
Using six of the folded pieces from Step One, fold the flaps down flat to create a slot. Slip one side of this slot over any one of the flaps on the cube. Next, slip the other side of the slot over its adjacent flap. Repeat on all six sides to complete the cube-shaped base.

④ **STEP FOUR: ASSEMBLE THE ROOF**
This step uses the remaining four folded pieces from Step One and three of the unfolded pieces. Fasten two folded pieces together by holding the pieces perpendicular, flaps facing each other, and slipping the flaps of one piece into the slots of the other, to create one connected pair. Create two of these pairs. Next, fold one of the unfolded pieces of paper in half and slip one of the long flaps into one of the slots in the first pair. Slip the other long flap into one of the slots in the second pair, to create a peak. Fold two more unfolded pieces in half and slip one of the pieces into the bottom left side of the peak and the other into the bottom right side of the peak. This creates two tabs on the bottom of the peaked roof. Attach the roof to the base by slipping the tabs of the peaked roof into slots on the cube-shaped base.

⑤ **STEP FIVE: ADD THE GABLES**
To create a gable to close the roof, begin by folding the remaining two pieces of paper in half, then folding one of the sides in half again. This creates a rigid flap on the bottom portion of the gable. Fold each of the two sides of the face of the gable inward to form a triangular peak; this fold also creates two triangular shaped flaps on the inside of the piece. Slip the double-folded flap on the bottom of the gable into the cube base and the two triangular flaps into the peaked roof.

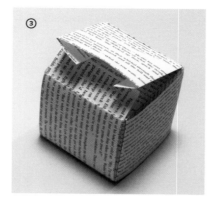

PROJECT NO.
{7}

Business Card Holder }

FOLDING BOOK PAGES IS A SIMPLE WAY TO CREATE three-dimensional bookish objects, such as this one-of-a-kind business card holder, which is bound to impress your literary colleagues. Alternate the size of your folded books to create a mail holder, an accessory to keep notes handy, or a clever work of art for your desk. Add a set of dates or alphabet tabs to the folded pages to create a daily reminder or address book.

Artist: Jason Thompson

✂ **MATERIALS**
book

💬 **CONSIDERATIONS**
This project is simple enough for children to enjoy. Any book will do, but paperbacks are a good option for the business card holder. Choose one with at least 100 pages. You'll need about fifteen minutes to fold one book. Don't worry about perfect folds; there are so many pages that a few imprecise folds won't be noticed.

PLAYING WITH BOOKS

①

INSTRUCTIONS:

① **FOLDING THE BOOK:**
Remove the front and back covers from a paperback book. This can usually be accomplished by carefully tearing the covers off by hand; no tools are necessary. Beginning with the first page, fold each book page in half toward the gutter. Depending on the number of pages, the thickness of the paper, and the grain direction of the pages, when completed, the book will be transformed into a half-cylinder shape. Lay the folded book on its side and place it on a decorative stand. It will fan out and sit flat.

··

❋ **TIPS:**
Two half cylinders stood on end and placed back to back creates a stand that can be used as a candleholder. By varying the folding process, such as folding pages at an angle, for example, you can create other three-dimensional shapes. Try folding the upper corner of a page down toward the bottom edge of the book page to create a triangle. Or alternate the folds: one page one way, the next page another way. Experiment. Fine artists use this technique to create all kinds of unique shapes.

Book pages folded and standing on end

Business card holder

Folded book pages

PROJECT NO. 8}

PAGE 40

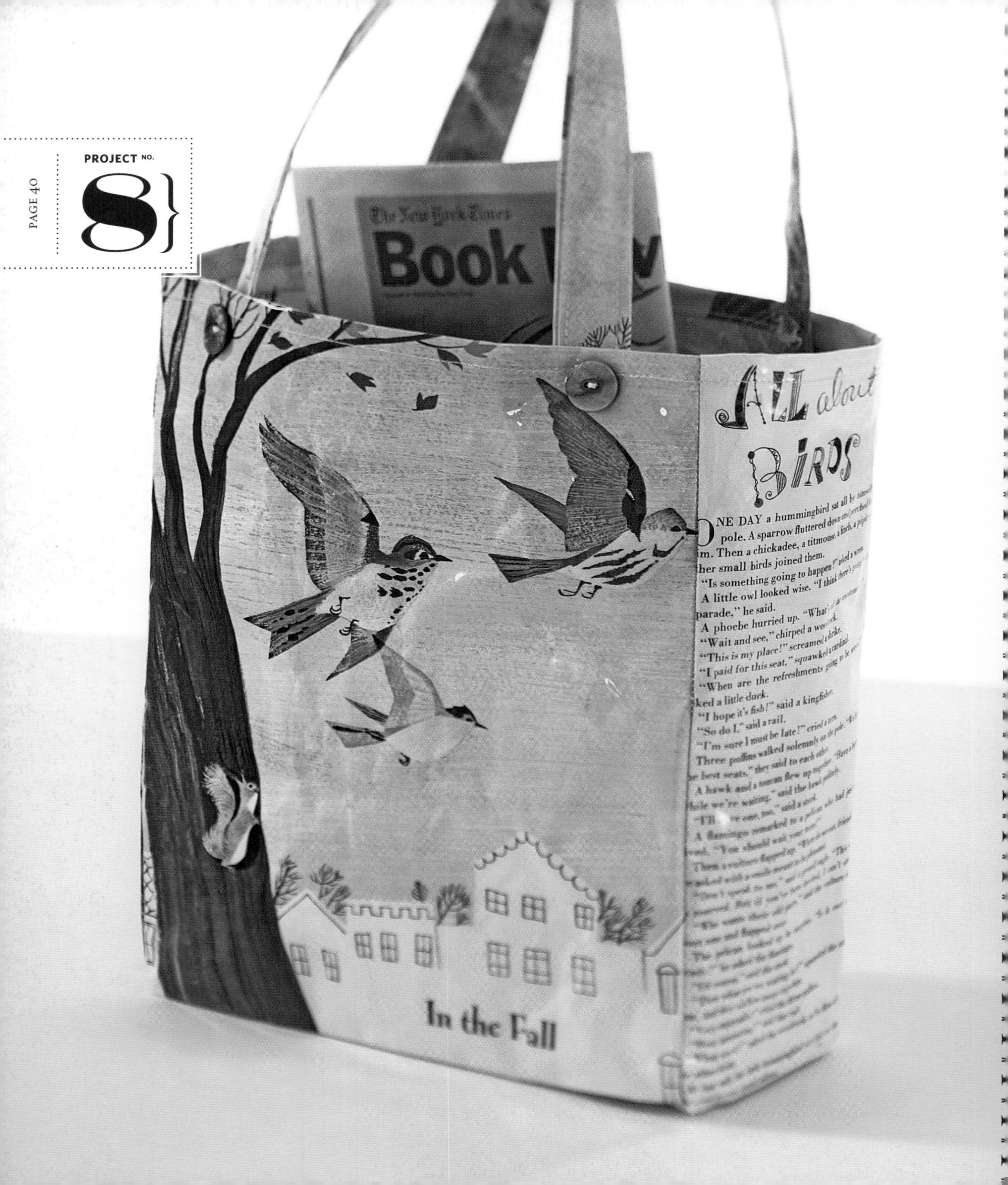

Book Bag

T HIS FUNKY, ONE-OF-A-KIND BOOK BAG was
designed using pages from a children's book featuring
animals and birds. The material has a texture similar
to reusable shopping bags and can be made using pages
from many types of printed matter, including comic books,
children's books, sheet music, art books, diaries, and ledgers.

Artist: Ilira Steinman

✂ **MATERIALS**
book pages
spray mount
lightweight clear vinyl
4 buttons
button-grade thread
hand needle
scissors
sewing machine

🗨 **CONSIDERATIONS**
This technique creates a laminated
paper-and-plastic material that can
be worked like fabric. The plastic
used for this project was purchased
from a local fabric store. Manufactured to protect furniture from dust
and stains, it is repurposed here to
waterproof and strengthen book
pages. We used the thinnest gauge
available. The finished bag will be
stiff enough to stand on its own;
it might crinkle and crease a little,
which is expected.

①

②

③

INSTRUCTIONS:

① **STEP ONE: CREATE THE MATERIAL**

Remove the decorative pages from a book by cutting or tearing them out. Lightly spray the front of the page with spray mount until the entire surface is covered. Adhere the paper to the plastic and smooth it with your hand to remove air bubbles and wrinkles. The spray mount will dry clear. Repeat the process by spraying the back of the paper (which now has plastic adhered to its front-facing side) and laminating it onto the plastic sheeting. Smooth and allow to dry. Trim off the extra plastic with scissors.

② **STEP TWO: CREATE A PATTERN**

No predesigned pattern was used for this bag—the dimensions of the paper pages dictated the overall size of the bag. The facing panels are full pages from the book, the sides are half pages, and the bottom is trimmed to fit. Alternatively, create a pattern by measuring the panels from a reusable shopping bag or other tote.

③ **STEP THREE: SEW THE BAG**

The material is easy to work with: Treat it just like fabric and sew it with a sewing machine. If you're designing a bag to carry heavy books or shopping goods, use a button-grade thread to sew the seams. The bag should be sewn inside out then turned right-side out when completed. To create the handles, fold strips of the laminated material slightly longer than the required handles. Attach the handles to the bag with buttons and button thread using a hand needle, then trim off excess plastic. Sew the handles securely if the bag is to be used for heavy books or groceries.

✸ **TIPS:**

Use the pages from a favorite novel and count on curious comments from your book-loving friends. The laminated pages can be used in place of fabric for other sewing projects such as hats, aprons, placemats, coasters, pocketbooks, and more. If the chosen pages are partially transparent—view them in sunlight to test them—they can be lined or laminated with a colored paper on the back before adhering them to the plastic sheeting.

Book bag created using book pages

Close-up of button and handle

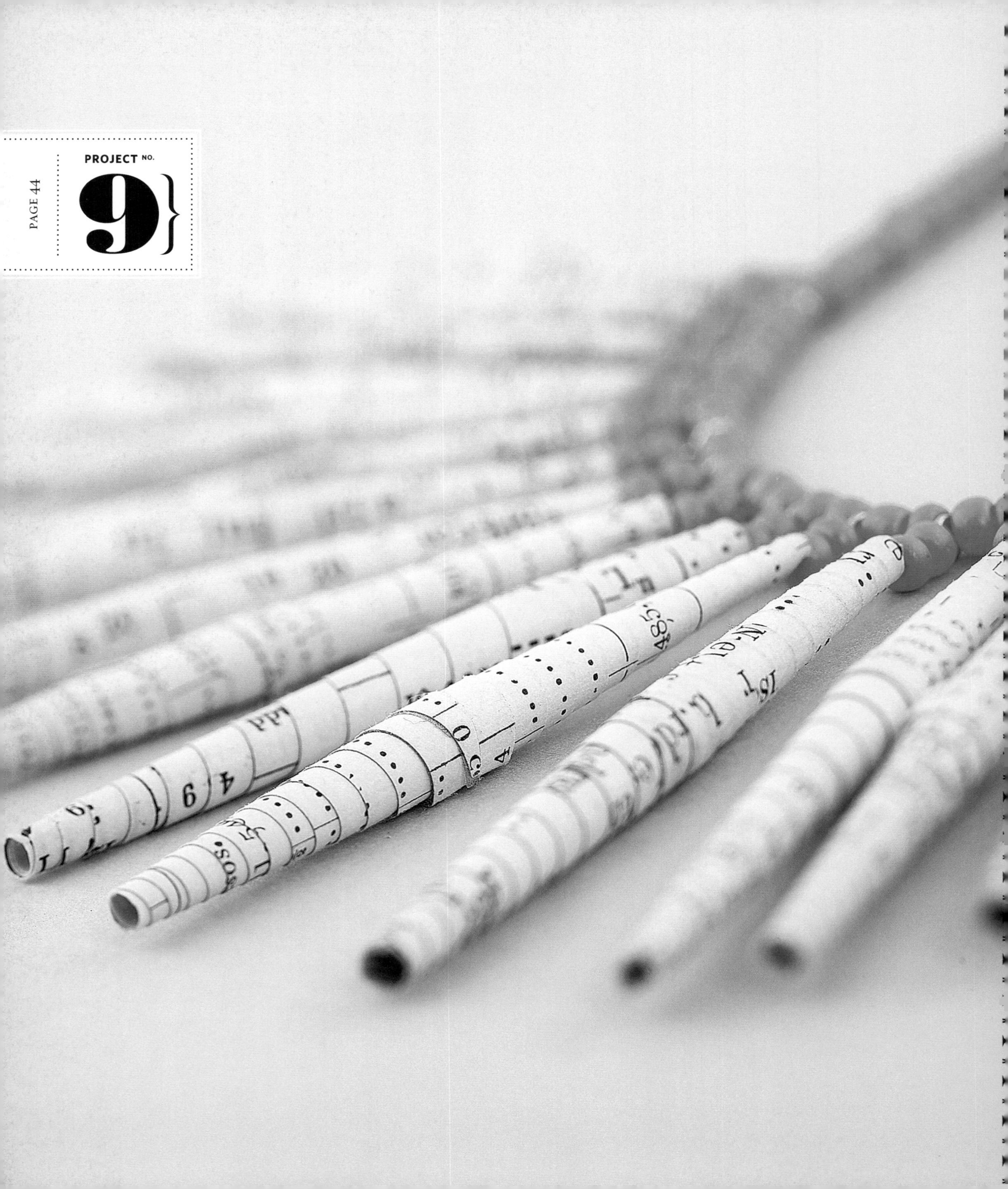

PAGE 44

PROJECT NO.

9

Beading is Fun

NECKLACES, BRACELETS, AND EARRINGS designed using book pages make a dramatic statement. Use the pages from your favorite books and proudly wear them to your next book club meeting or book signing. The beads are easy to create and can be rolled into various thicknesses and lengths.

Artist: Jason Thompson

✂ MATERIALS
book pages
rolling tool
white glue
glue brush
polyurethane (optional)
jeweler's beads
wire cutters
crimping tool

FOR NECKLACE:
Jewelry wire, crimps, and hooks

FOR BRACELET:
Safety pins and flexible elastic

FOR EARRINGS:
Jewelry wire and earring findings

🗩 CONSIDERATIONS
The beads are easy to create by simply rolling paper triangles around a rolling tool. To vary the sizes of the beads, adjust the widest point of the triangular strip of book paper. I got a little fancy with the necklace pictured here by designing and printing templates for the triangular book page strips using a computer and printer. This allowed me to create beads of progressively larger sizes to exact specifications. The strips were printed directly onto the book pages and then cut out by hand.

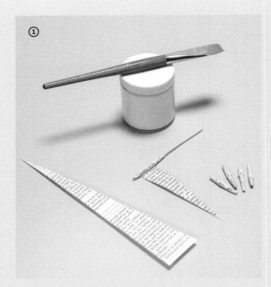

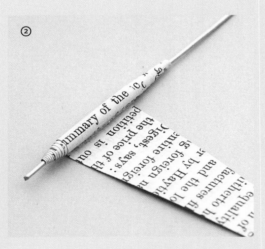

INSTRUCTIONS:

① STEP ONE: CUT THE PAPER

Use book pages with interesting patterns, such as images, typography, or even a ledger book from the 1800s, which is used for the jewelry in these examples. Trim a book page into a long triangular shape, for example, 10" (25.4 cm) long and 2" (5.1 cm) wide at one end, tapering to a point at the other end. These dimensions can be varied for different sizes of beads—however, maintain the point at one end.

② STEP TWO: ROLL THE BEAD

These beads have a narrow center hole, so use a thin rolling tool, such as a knitting needle, a piece of thin wire, or even a sewing needle. Paper bead–winding tools designed specifically for rolling paper beads are available. These tools are helpful but not necessary, because common items found in any household can be used to roll paper beads.

Using the rolling tool, begin rolling the bead at the wider end of the strip—in this example, the 2" (5.1 cm) end—around the rolling tool. Continue rolling the paper until the pointed end is almost reached. Stop rolling with 1.5" (3.8 cm) of the point left exposed and liberally apply white glue along the point. Glue can be applied directly from the bottle using an applicator tip or with a brush.

Once the adhesive is on the paper, finish rolling the bead. The adhesive will extrude and smear, but this is okay. Continue spinning the completed bead, using your fingers to coat the entire outside of the bead with white glue. This final step keeps the bead from unrolling. Paper beads can also be coated with a clear polyurethane.

③ STEP THREE: CREATE THE JEWELRY

The finished book-page paper beads can be used in place of jeweler's beads to create various styles of decorative jewelry. String a necklace by inserting a wire and a colorful jeweler's bead through the center of the paper bead and attaching it to necklace wire. Space the paper beads with jeweler's beads along the necklace wire, and secure the beads with crimps and hooks.

Create a bracelet by inserting paper beads onto the pin side of safety pins. String the safety pins onto elastic beading cord and space with colorful beads. Create an earring by slipping a wire and colorful bead through the center of the paper bead and attaching it to earring findings. All of these materials can be found at local art and bead stores.

✴ TIPS:

Many books have been written on jewelry making and metalsmithing, which describe in more detail the techniques used to make jewelry. I invite the reader to use additional resources and to learn jewelry making in detail. The three pieces shown here were designed and created by simply experimenting with paper beads and beadmaking supplies, such as wire, crimps, beads, and wire cutters. Experiment and have fun.

Tools and materials used to create the paper bead necklace

Close-up of paper bead necklace

Tools and materials used to create the paper bead bracelet

Close-up of paper bead bracelet

Tools and materials used to create the paper bead earrings

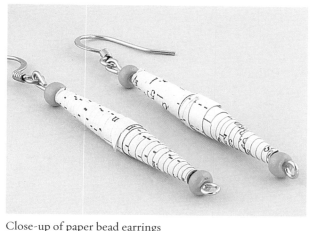

Close-up of paper bead earrings

Book to Bloom

U SE BOOK PAGES TO CREATE A SPRAY of delicate blossoms secured to natural sticks and stems. Create a permanent and sophisticated floral arrangement to display in a slender vase.

Artist: Sheila Daniels

✄ **MATERIALS**
book pages
scissors
natural stem
wire
powdered chalk

💬 **CONSIDERATIONS**
The powdered chalk used for this project is similar to blush makeup. The light application creates a soft pink glow, similar to a new blossom. These instructions describe how to create small blossoms. Experiment by varying the size of the book pages to create larger blossoms.

①

②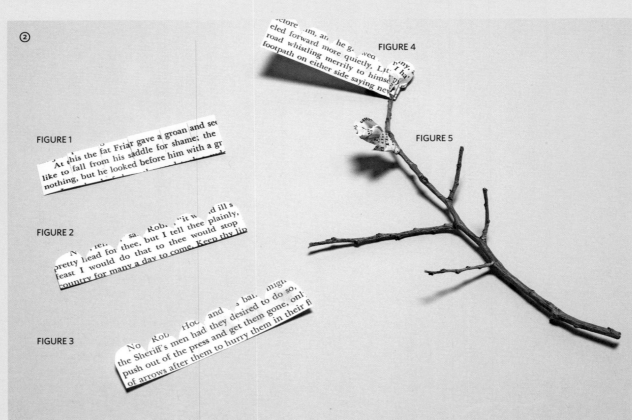

FIGURE 4

FIGURE 1

FIGURE 2

FIGURE 3

FIGURE 5

INSTRUCTIONS:

① **STEP ONE: CUT TO SIZE**
Beginning with a book page cut to 0.75" × 3" (2 × 7.6 cm), make five short cuts along the length of the page, being careful to avoid cutting through the entire strip (figure 1). Round the corners of the cuts with scissors (figure 2). Lightly coat each of the rounded tabs with powdered chalk (figure 3). These five chalked tabs will each create a separate petal in Step Two.

② **STEP TWO: SECURE THE BLOSSOMS**
Place one end of the paper strip onto the tip of a natural stem and carefully roll it around the stem (figure 4). Be sure the side with the powdered chalk is on the inside. Roll the paper strip completely around the stem (figure 5).

③ **STEP THREE: OPEN THE PETALS**
Tie a small length of wire around the base of the blossom to secure it in place. The wire will hold the base of the blossom securely around the stem. Carefully spread the petals outward to expose the powdered chalk side of the paper. The wire will hold the petals in place.

✳ TIPS:
Use different colors of chalk for the petals. Vary the stems for fuller bouquets. The process can be used to create petals and blossoms of any size.

Blossoms in vase

PROJECT NO.

11}

Gifting

CREATE BOWS, TAGS, AND WRAPPING PAPER using book pages with interesting patterns, such as musical notations, illustrations, or pages printed in a foreign language.

Artist: Jason Thompson

✂ **MATERIALS**
book pages
laminating adhesive and heavier
  material (for tags)
white glue (optional, for wrapping
  paper)
double-sided tape
scissors
shaped die punch (optional)

💬 **CONSIDERATIONS**
Book pages are small in relation to
commercially available wrapping
paper, the surface area hardly
large enough to wrap a bar of soap
(the item wrapped in the example
here). Larger sheets of book-page
wrapping paper can be created by
tiling several sheets together using
double-sided tape or white glue.

PLAYING WITH BOOKS

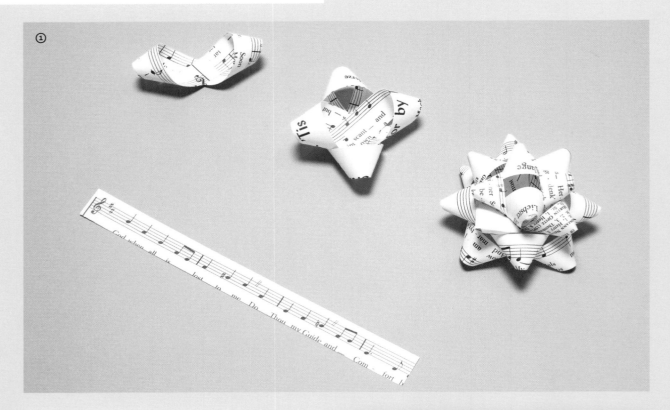

INSTRUCTIONS:

① **PROJECT ONE: BOWS**

Bows are constructed using five identically formed book-page strips. Begin with a strip of paper cut to 0.75" × 7" (2 × 17.8 cm). Place a square of double-sided tape in the exact center of the strip. Carefully curve one end of the strip toward the center by looping and rotating it 180 degrees, then firmly adhere the end to the center of the strip. This loop should curve toward the center of the strip at an angle. Complete the process by creating a second loop with the other end of the strip. Repeat to create five looped pieces. Using double-sided tape, adhere the five pieces on top of one another, rotating each one to fit inside the one below. As the layers are progressively assembled, the bow will take shape.

② **PROJECT TWO: TAGS**

Cut the tags from book pages by hand or by punching them out using a shaped die. Design your hand-cut tags to any shape. TIP: Laminate a heavier material onto the book pages before shaping them to create a sturdier tag.

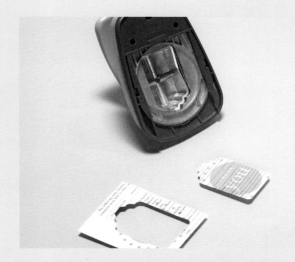

③ **PROJECT THREE: WRAPPING PAPER**

Using book pages as wrapping paper is straightforward. Create larger sheets by adhering several book pages together using double sided tape or white glue. TIP: Thoughtfully select specific pages to wrap specific gifts. Use notated sheet music to wrap a gift for a musician. Foreign-language book pages can be used to wrap a going-away gift. Use the pages from children's books to wrap gifts for new moms and little ones.

PAGE 56

PROJECT NO.

12}

Kusudama

CREATE AN ORNAMENTAL ORIGAMI FLOWER using five book pages. Flowers can be used as decorative elements, ornaments, in place of gift bows, as floral arrangements, or as placecards for a table setting, as shown in this project.

Artist: Jason Thompson

✂ **MATERIALS**
book pages
white glue
glue brush

💬 **CONSIDERATIONS**
Use the images and the instructions together to learn the folds. Once perfected, the flower is quick and easy to assemble. This project is suitable for kids to enjoy. There are only six folds and one adhesive step per petal. Five petals are needed to make a flower.

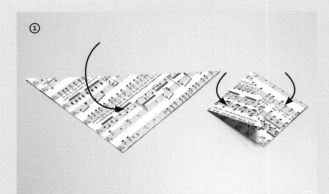

Fold 1   Fold 2

Fold 3   Fold 4

Fold 5   Fold 6

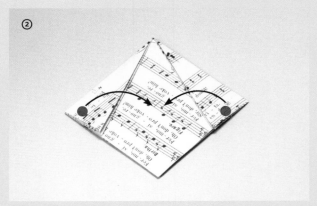

Apply adhesive

Glue the petal together

Join petals together to create flower

INSTRUCTIONS:

① **STEP ONE: MAKE THE FOLDS**

Begin with five pieces of book pages cut to 6" × 6" (15.2 × 15.2 cm). Fold 1: Fold the square into a triangle. Fold 2: Fold the two creased corners down to create a smaller square. Fold 3: Fold the two triangular flaps in half. Fold 4: Open these flaps up, then re-fold them flat, so that the inner crease created in Fold 3 falls to the outside. Fold 5: Fold the tips up. Fold 6: Fold the triangular flaps in half inward. The final shape of the paper after these six folds will be a square.

② **STEP TWO: CREATE THE PETAL**

To create a petal, the folded piece must be rolled inward. Apply white glue to the flaps with a glue brush; carefully roll the petal and press the two flaps together. Allow the adhesive to tack up. Repeat Steps One and Two to create five petals.

Joining five petals together will create one Kusudama flower. Apply a strip of adhesive to the inner crease of one petal and adhere a second petal to the adhesive. Once these two petals have been joined, continue the process to join five petals together.

❋ **TIPS:**

Japanese Kusudama were originally created using bunches of flowers or herbs rolled into cloth balls and were used like incense or potpourri to dispel evil spirits and disease. The word Kusudama is a combination of two Japanese words *kusuri* (medicine) and *tama* (ball). Kusudama are now typically created with paper and are used as decorations or as gifts.

Close-up of Kusudama flower used as a table marker

Three Kusudama flowers

The Time Machine }

ALMOST ANY HARDCOVER OR PAPERBACK BOOK can be used for this project. Choose a title that complements the topic of "time," a book cover with an interesting design, or a favorite book or cover.

Artist: Jason Thompson

✂ MATERIALS
book
electric drill
clock mechanism
clock numbers (optional)
bookend (optional)

💬 CONSIDERATIONS
Clock mechanisms, available at craft stores and online, are manufactured with varying shaft lengths. Measure the entire thickness of the book before shopping for a clock mechanism. TIP: Clock hands are often interchangeable. Replace the hands that come with the clock mechanism with those from another clock, if desired.

INSTRUCTIONS:

① **STEP ONE: DRILL AND ATTACH THE CLOCK**

Drill a hole through the book using a power drill. Insert the shaft of the clock mechanism from the back of the book through the hole and secure it with the accompanying washers and nuts. Attach the hands to the face following the instructions provided with the clock mechanism. If desired, attach clock numbers to the face of the book.

② **STEP TWO: OPTIONAL BOOK STAND**

Although most hardcover books will stand upright on their own, paperbacks can require a little help. To stand a paperback vertically, slip the book over a bookend before attaching the clock mechanism. The stand should not be visible from the front of the book with the clock face.

❋ **TIPS:**

Select the correct drill bit diameter by following the instructions on the clock mechanism packaging. Drill clean holes through the front and back book covers by placing the book between scraps of wood before drilling. Be sure the clock mechanism is tightly secured to the book; any wobble or rotation of the clock mechanism will result in inaccurate time.

Paperback book with clock mechanism. The book is sitting on a hidden bookend so that it remains upright.

Roll Your Own Mat

PAPER ROLLS CREATE STRUCTURAL ELEMENTS that can be used to create mats, coasters, table runners, desk accessories, and even three-dimensional containers. The process used to connect the tubes together results in an extremely strong connection.

Artist: Jason Thompson

✂ **MATERIALS**
book pages
rolling tool
white glue
glue brush
bobby pins

🗩 **CONSIDERATIONS**
Use tightly rolled tubes of paper pages to create a unique tabletop mat. Paper pages can be rolled vertically or horizontally, each creating a different pattern. Practice with different pages and orientations before creating a large number of rolls. Bobby pins are available in different sizes—smaller is better for this application.

① ② ③

INSTRUCTIONS:

① **STEP ONE: GATHER THE MATERIALS**
Begin with book pages cut to 8" × 8" (20.3 × 20.3 cm) (this dimension can be varied for different projects). Use a rolling tool, such as a dowel, to roll the paper pages. The tool should have a uniform diameter across its entire length to create evenly rolled tubes.

② **STEP TWO: CREATE THE ROLLS**
Beginning at one edge, roll the pages evenly around the rolling tool. Apply white glue with a glue brush to the final edge of the paper page, then complete the roll. Allow the adhesive to tack up before sliding the paper roll off the rolling tool. Create twenty rolls.

③ **STEP THREE: ASSEMBLE**
Once the rolls are dry, hold two together and slide a bobby pin through the center of each to fasten the two rolls together. Repeat this process at the other end of the rolls. Continue securing additional rolls to one another using the bobby pins. TIP: To reduce the visibility of the bobby pins in the completed piece, push them into the center of the rolls as tightly as possible.

✳ **TIP:**
Create a decorative pencil holder by attaching the first and last paper rolls together and placing the cylinder shape over a metal can.

Close-up of rolled mat

Close-up of rolled container

Artist: Jason Thompson

Dimensional Circle Ornaments

Create a unique book-page ornament using book pages and a circle cutter.

INSTRUCTIONS:

① **STEP ONE: CUT AND FOLD**
Using a circle cutter, cut twenty circles from book pages (a 2" [5.1 cm] circle cutter was used for this project). Use cardboard to create an equilateral triangle template that fits exactly within the circumference of the circle. Place this triangle in the center of the circle and trace the three sides onto the circle. Use these traced lines as guides for folding the tabs on the circles. TIP: Fold the tabs so the traced lines are on the inside of the ornament.

② **STEP TWO: HATS AND STRIPS**
Adhere five pieces together, as shown below, to create a hat-shaped dome. Repeat to make a second hat-shaped dome. Adhere the final ten pieces together in a strip, as shown below, center.

③ **STEP THREE: ASSEMBLE**
Turn the strip into a hoop by adhering the first and last tabs of the strip together. Attach the hat-shaped dome to one side of the hoop. Attach the second hat-shaped dome to the other side of the hoop. Use binder clips to hold the half-finished sphere together while gluing the tabs.

TIPS:
Alternate colored paper with book pages to design spheres that coordinate with each other. Use a computer to print an equilateral triangle with the same diameter as the circle, and use the printout as a template by tracing it onto the cardboard.

Close-up of a paper page ornament assembled using twenty paper circles

✂ MATERIALS

book pages	cardboard
circle cutter	pencil
white glue	binder clips
glue brush	

🗨 CONSIDERATIONS
The basic shape used to design this ornament is a triangle, which is traced inside a circle. Create larger or smaller ornaments by varying the size of the circles.

PROJECT NO.
16}

Punched Paper Ornaments

S EVERAL STRIPS ARE FANNED OUT to create a spherical ornament. No adhesive is required.

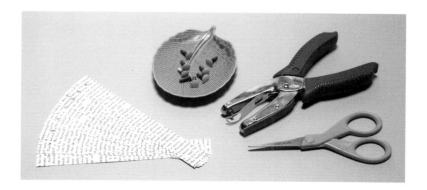

Close-up of an ornament created using nine strips of book page paper and two rivets

INSTRUCTIONS:

① **STEP ONE: CUT AND PUNCH**
Cut eight strips of book pages to 0.5" × 4" (1.3 × 10.2 cm). Punch a hole at both ends of each strip. The hole should be large enough to accept a paper fastener or rivet.

② **STEP TWO: AFFIX AND FAN**
Place a rivet or paper fastener through the holes in one end of the eight strips. Place a second rivet or paper fastener into the holes at the other end of the eight strips. Fan out the strips—the strips will form a sphere as the pieces are fanned out—so that they are situated at

equal distances along the circumference of the sphere. Compression will hold the ornament together; however, paper fasteners can be used to permanently hold the spherical shape.

☀ **TIP:**
Adhere a small circle of paper over the rivet or paper fastener (or between the strips and the fastner as shown) to give the ornament a finished look.

Artist: Jason Thompson

✂ **MATERIALS**
book pages
scissors
hole punch
rivets or paper fasteners

☞ **CONSIDERATIONS**
Smaller spheres require fewer strips; larger spheres require more strips.

Sewn Paper Ornaments }

U SE A CIRCLE CUTTER AND SEWING MACHINE to create spherical ornaments of varying sizes.

INSTRUCTIONS:

① **STEP ONE: CUT**
Using a circle cutter, cut circles from book pages. The largest ornament pictured here is 4" (10.2 cm) in diameter, the smallest is 2" (5.1 cm) in diameter.

② **STEP TWO: SEW AND FAN**
Create a stack of at least twelve circles and sew them together by stitching down the center of the circles. Once sewn, fan the ornament open.

⚹ **TIPS:**
Leave a foot of trailing thread remaining on each ornament. Use this extra thread to hang the ornaments. Layer colorful paper circles between the book pages to create one-of-a-kind ornaments.

Close-up of a sewn paper ornament

Artist: Jason Thompson

✂ **MATERIALS**
book pages
circle cutter or scissors
sewing machine

💬 **CONSIDERATIONS**
The circles can be cut to any size. Larger ornaments are easier to fan open than smaller ones. Use at least twelve circles per ornament.

PROJECT NO.

18}

Basket Case

CREATE A PAPER BASKET USING 264 PIECES OF PAPER. This project is easy enough for kids and clever adults, but bring a basket-full of patience—you'll need it; the process is easy, but the shapes take time to create. The resulting basket is an attractive container for knitting supplies, plush dolls, yesterday's mail, or chocolate treats.

Artist: Jason Thompson

✂ MATERIALS
264 book page strips
cardboard for base
patience

💬 CONSIDERATIONS
This technique is popular among campers—so says a crafty camping friend. Once kids perfect lanyard bracelet crafts, they move on to creating necklaces out of candy wrappers with this interlocking folded paper technique. Who knew? Stick to the vintage paper pages for a more sophisticated project.

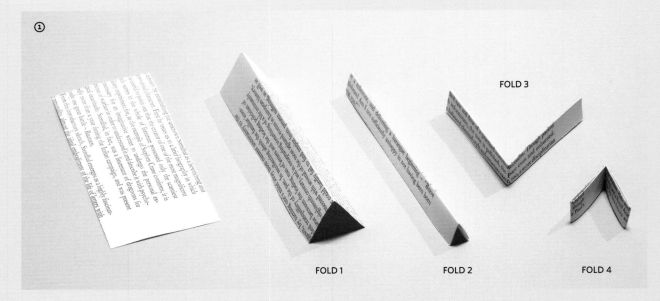

FOLD 3

FOLD 1   FOLD 2   FOLD 4

①

②

③

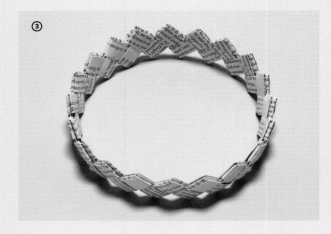

INSTRUCTIONS:

① **STEP ONE: FOLDING THE SHAPES**
Four folds are needed to create the interlocking paper shapes. Begin with book pages cut to 2" × 5" (5.1 × 12.7 cm). Fold 1: Fold in half lengthwise to 1" × 5" (2.5 × 12.7 cm). Fold 2: Fold in half lengthwise again to 0.5 × 5" (1.3 × 12.7 cm). Fold 3: Fold in half to create a V shape. Fold 4: Finally, fold each end inward toward the crease in the bottom of the V to create a smaller V. That's it. These folded pieces of paper are the basic shapes that lock into each other to form the rigid sides of the basket. Folding the paper shapes is easy, but it takes time to fold enough to make a basket, so have patience.

② **STEP TWO: INTERLOCKING THE PIECES**
To lock the two V-shaped pieces together, insert the two tabs (top of the Vs) of one of the pieces into the two slots in a second piece. They will slip into each other and lock together. Once two pieces are locked together, insert a third and repeat this process to create strips of interlocking pieces.

③ **STEP THREE: WEAVING STRIPS AND CIRCLES**
Lock together forty-four paper shapes to create one complete strip. This strip is turned into a circle by interlocking the first and last tabs together. The technique to

lock these last two pieces together is the same technique used to lock the individual pieces. However, the tabs at one end of the strip will need to be reopened to fit into the slots in the piece at the other end of the strip. This final step will turn the strip into a circle.

④ **STEP FOUR: FINISHING THE BASKET**
Six stacked completed circles will create the sides of the basket. To secure the circles together, weave a piece of folded paper (Folds 1 and 2 in Step One) through successive layers. This can be done on the outside of the basket, because the ends of this weaving strip will be hidden by the folded tabs that make up the circular rings. The base inside the basket was created using a circular piece of cardboard cut to size and then fitted into the bottom of the basket—no glue or other means of adhering the base is necessary; compression will hold it securely to the bottom of the basket.

✴ **TIPS:**
The ratio between the width and length of the pieces of paper used to make the interlocking shapes is 2:5. Using this ratio, other sizes of paper can be calculated and folded into larger or smaller interlocking pieces. Larger folded shapes will create a basket that is quicker to assemble but possibly less flexible. This interlocking paper technique has been used to create other functional objects, such as bags, purses, placemats, and even a paper prom dress!

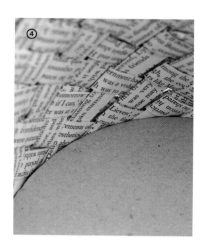

Close-up of the woven paper basket. The entire basket is created using book pages trimmed and folded to a single size.

The Book Mobile

D ESIGN YOUR VERY OWN HANGING MOBILE using butterfly-shaped book pages. It's easy to create any number of shapes to flutter in the breeze: birds, hearts, teardrops, letters, numbers, circles, stars, and more.

Artist: Mollie C. Greene

✂ MATERIALS
book pages
scissors
hole punch
cardboard
thread
white glue
glue brush

🖎 CONSIDERATIONS
Pages can be cut into numerous shapes, sizes, and lengths. A book cover can be used in place of the star-shaped platform from which the mobile hangs. For example, cut out bird shapes to hang from a hard cover taken from a book about birds.

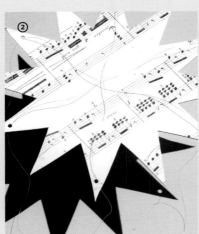

INSTRUCTIONS:

① STEP ONE: CUT THE SHAPES

Cut the butterfly shapes from paper pages. TIP: Use a cardboard template to cut several identical butterflies by tracing the outline of the template onto the book pages. Create at least eighteen butterflies to attach to six strands. The number, size, and shape of the butterflies can be varied for different mobiles.

② STEP TWO: CREATE THE PLATFORM

Cut out the platform from which the strands will hang. In this example, the platform is cut into a star shape using cardboard similar to that used to back notebooks. TIP: The cardboard can be laminated with book pages on both sides before cutting out the star shape. Use a hole punch to create six holes in the platform; the thread will be strung through the holes. Regardless of the shape of the platform, be sure to punch an even number of regularly spaced holes around the platform. Once the holes have been punched, string thread through two opposite holes, leaving at least 24" (61 cm) of string hanging from each. Repeat for all the holes. TIP: String the thread up from the bottom of the platform, across the top of the platform and down through the opposite hole.

③ STEP THREE: ATTACH THE SHAPES

Using a dab of white glue, which will dry clear, attach the butterflies to the thread. Begin with the uppermost butterfly and work down the thread, spacing each butterfly approximately 6" (15.2 cm) apart.

Attach all of the butterflies at one time by placing the platform onto a large work surface and fanning out the strands of thread. Once the butterflies have been attached, trim any remaining thread extending beyond the bottom-most butterfly. Secure the six strands to the top of the platform with a spot of glue.

④ **STEP FOUR: HANG AND BALANCE**
The final steps will create a loop from which to hang the mobile and will balance it. Create the loop by stringing thread through two of the holes in the platform but looping the thread above the platform. The longer the loop, the less likely it is that the platform will wobble, so use a length of thread appropriate for the location from which the mobile will be hung. Once a loop has been created, hang the mobile. More than likely, the platform for the mobile will tilt in one direction. To remedy this, cut out small cardboard shapes from the scraps leftover from the platform. Place these shapes on top of the platform, adjusting the placement until the platform is balanced, then use a small amount of glue to permanently adhere the balance weights.

✱ **TIPS:**
Create a book mobile for a baby's room using a children's book. Use heart shapes for a romantic mobile. For a colorful mobile, back the paper pages with colored paper before cutting out the shapes. This is a great project for creative kids.

Close-up of the butterfly book mobile

PROJECT NO.

20}

Immobile Mobile

CREATE FLUTTERY BUTTERFLY SHAPES using wire, adhesive, and book pages. Carefully nudge the wire ends into birthday cakes, cupcakes, and other tasty desserts to brighten a festive setting.

Artist: Mollie C. Greene

✂ MATERIALS
book pages
wire
adhesive
scissors

🗨 CONSIDERATIONS
Precut floral wire can be used in place of spooled wire. Clean the wire with alcohol before placing it into food items. Other paper shapes to consider are bees, stars, letters, numbers (for birthdays), clouds, hearts, and more. Use your imagination.

①

②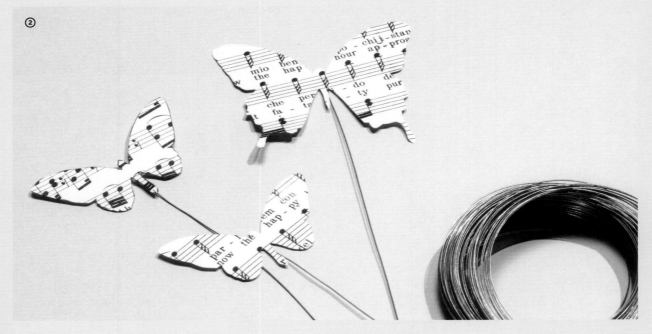

INSTRUCTIONS:

① **STEP ONE: TRACE AND CUT**
Draw directly onto the book pages and use a pair of scissors to cut out the butterfly shapes. Or use a cardboard template to create several butterflies of the same shape and size. Use pages from printed matter such as musical notation books, comic books, and illustrations.

② **STEP TWO: AFFIX TO THE WIRE**
Cut a piece of thin wire (24-gauge, for example) 6" to 8" (15.2 to 20.3 cm) long, depending on your application. Affix the butterfly shapes to the wire using a spot of clear-drying adhesive, such as PVA. Allow it to dry, then have fun decorating.

✳ **TIPS:**
Use two identical shapes and sandwich the wire between the two to hide the adhesive. Wire can be affixed to floral bouquets for a whimsical butterfly arrangement.

Place the butterflies into bouquets by wrapping the wire around the flower stems.

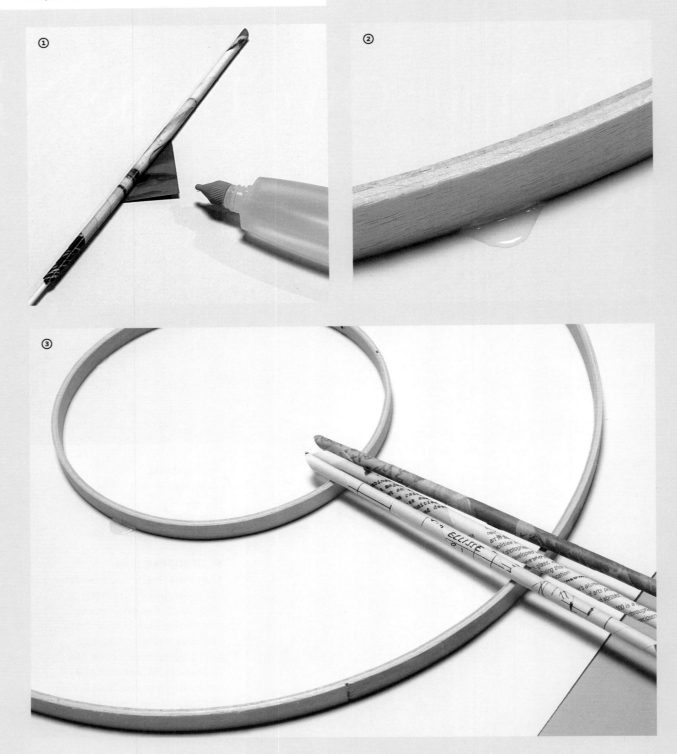

INSTRUCTIONS:

① STEP ONE: CREATE THE ROLLS

Begin with book pages cut to 5.5" × 5.5" (14 × 14 cm). Because the pages are rolled from corner to corner, this sheet size will result in a roll 8" (20.3 cm) long. Use a rolling tool approximately ¼" (6 mm) in diameter, such as a paint brush handle, chopstick, or thin metal rod. Begin rolling at one corner and roll the page tightly around the rolling tool. Stop rolling about 2" (5.1 cm) from the opposite corner and apply adhesive to the corner. Finish rolling and allow the glue to set for a few seconds before releasing. Repeat to create approximately 125 rolls.

② STEP TWO: PREPARE THE WORK SURFACE

Temporarily attach the two wooden embroidery hoops to the work surface by placing a spot of glue on both the hoops and work surface at the 12, 9, 6, and 3 o'clock points. The hoops will be removed from the work surface once the starburst frame is completed, but this initial step secures both hoops at an equal distance from each other while the paper rolls are being attached.

③ STEP THREE: ATTACH THE ROLLS

Using clear glue, attach the paper rolls to the hoops. Clear glue in an applicator tube works well for this step. Begin by gluing the first roll to both the inner and outer hoops so that the roll extends beyond the outer hoop. Continue attaching the rolls one at a time all the way around the hoop. TIP: Dry-fit the last dozen rolls to be sure the spacing allows for the last roll to fit snugly next to the first roll.

✳ TIPS:

Add a mirror by using adjustable wooden embroidery hoops. Before attaching the paper rolls, loosen the adjustable screw of the inner hoop. Once the rolls are attached and the adhesive has dried, fit a circular mirror into the inner hoop and secure it by tightening the screw until the hoop holds the mirror in place. Round mirrors can be found at craft stores and online. You can use this same technique to create a clock by securing a round piece of board into the inner hoop and setting the clock mechanism into the center of the board.

Close-up of paper rolls

Close-up of paper rolls

Pyramid Gift Box

}

P RESENT THIS BOOK PAGE–covered gift box as a housewarming or holiday gift. The sides of the pyramid can be covered with paper pages for specific occasions; for example, use interior-design book pages for a housewarming present or cookbook pages for a dinner-party gift.

Artist: Jason Thompson

✂ **MATERIALS**
book pages
chipboard
artist tape
PVA glue
hole punch
scissors
decorative ribbon

💬 **CONSIDERATIONS**
Isosceles triangles, which have two equal sides, are used to create this box. The length and width of the triangles can vary, as long as they remain symmetrical and the length of the shortest sides matches the length of the base. The chipboard triangles can be covered with book pages before assembly; in this example, they are wrapped with musical notation pages.

① ②

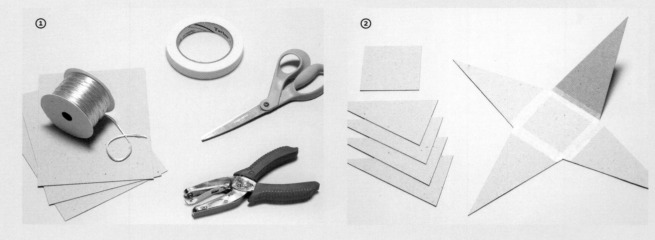

③

INSTRUCTIONS:

① **STEP ONE: MEASURE AND CUT**

Create the base by cutting chipboard to an exact square. Any size will do, as long as it is perfectly square. The pyramid in the example has a 3" × 3" (7.6 × 7.6 cm) base. Create the triangular sides by cutting chipboard into four identical triangles. The bottom of each triangle must be cut to the same size as the base—in this example, 3" (7.6 cm). TIP: Cut the first triangular piece and use it as a template for the other three sides.

② **STEP TWO: ASSEMBLE THE PYRAMID**

Attach the first triangular piece by hinging it onto the base using artist tape. Trim off any extra tape, if necessary. Once the four triangles have been attached, stand them together to form the pyramid. The four sides should meet and stand on their own. Next, cover the chipboard material with book pages using PVA glue. Press flat beneath a stack of heavy books and allow to dry before moving to step three.

③ **STEP THREE: ADD THE RIBBON**

Punch a hole into the top of each triangle with a hole punch. Thread a 12" (30.5 cm) length of decorative ribbon through the four holes. Lace the ribbon into the first hole, out through the second, and repeat for the third and fourth holes. Pull tight and create a loop on the trailing end of the ribbon. This ribbon will hold the pyramid closed, allowing items to be safely placed and transported inside the pyramid box.

TIPS:

Create pyramid gift boxes using book covers for the base material, in place of chipboard, or for the decorative panels. Pyramid boxes also make beautiful ornaments.

Close-up of pyramid gift box

The Circle Game

CREATE A DRAMATIC DISK NECKLACE using pages from a favorite book. The completed project is stylish and elegant, and the process is simple enough for kids to accomplish in an afternoon.

Artist: Jason Thompson

✂ MATERIALS
book pages
hole punch
circle punch
necklace materials

🗨 CONSIDERATIONS
Create color variations in the necklace by alternating groups of circles from different books. Alternate circle sizes to create varying strands. The more circles used in the necklace, the more dramatic it will appear. Choose the book carefully: chances are, someone will want to know which book was used—and why.

①

②

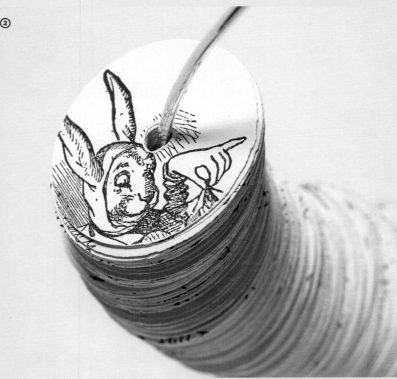

INSTRUCTIONS:

① **STEP ONE: PAPER PAGES TO PAPER CIRCLES**

Punch the hole in the center of the circles before punching the circles themselves. The hole in the center of the circle is like a hole in a bead, the closer it is to the center, the more symmetrical the final necklace will appear. Use a circle punch (available in various diameters) to complete the circular paper beads. Hold the circle punch upside down, so that you can see that the punched hole is accurately centered in the circle.

② **STEP TWO: STRING THE BEADS**

String the paper beads onto the necklace material: string, leather, or wire. The paper circles can be spaced with beads or other decorative elements.

✹ **TIP:**

Paper pages from old books can crack or crease. Punch a few circles and handle for a moment before going ahead with the project, to be sure the paper circles don't tear.

Close-up of necklace made with circles cut from book pages created by Nicci Cobb

Book page paper necklace created by Nicci Cobb

Book page paper necklace

PROJECT NO.

24}

Playing with Books

}

U SE TWO IDENTICAL BOOKS to create a one-of-a-kind matching game. Ask a child to collaborate by choosing the images to appear on the pieces and to help punch the circles from book pages.

Artist: Jason Thompson

✄ **MATERIALS**
book pages
two identical illustrated books
decorative paper
circle cutter
artist tape
white glue or dry mount adhesive
glue brush

💬 **CONSIDERATIONS**
Ask the folks at used-book stores for additional copies of popular children's titles. Second-hand books by popular authors such as Dr. Seuss, Margaret Wise Brown, Eric Carle, and Maurice Sendak are often available.

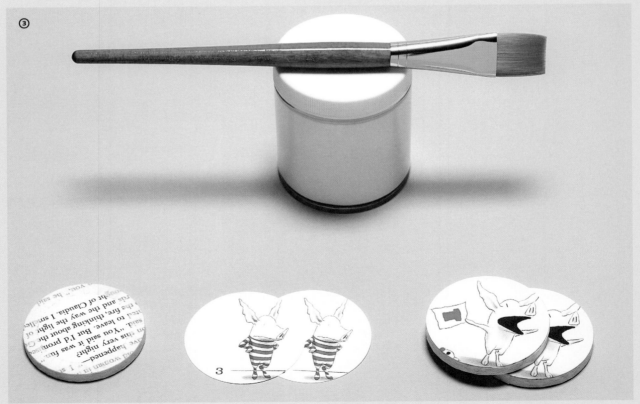

INSTRUCTIONS:

① STEP ONE: GATHER AND CUT THE MATERIALS

Use a book with thick pages, such as a hardcover novel, and cut 2" (5.1 cm) circles with a circle cutter. Cut enough circles to create thirty-two circle stacks approximately ¼" (6 mm) high. Using the same circle cutter, cut sixteen pairs of identical illustrations from each of the children's books; each pair of cut-outs will be affixed to the front of the 2" (5.1 cm) circle stacks to create a pair of matching game pieces. Finally, cut thirty-two 2" (5.1 cm) circle shapes from decorative paper. These decorative circles will be affixed to the back of the game pieces.

② STEP TWO: CREATE THE PIECES

Wrap ¾" (1.9 cm) artist tape around the circumference of each ¼" (6 mm) stack of paper pages. Fold the artist tape down over the top and bottom layers of the stacks. The tape will hold the paper circles together and form the playing pieces. You should have 32 playing pieces.

③ STEP THREE: COVER THE PIECES

Use white glue or a dry-mount method to adhere the illustrations to the front of the pieces and the decorative paper to the back. Be sure to create two identical sets of playing pieces, so the pieces can be matched.

✸ TIPS:

The playing pieces can be used for other games such as Dao, Checkers, and Go. Use the same process to create two sets of playing pieces using two different books. Ask a child to make up his or her own board game.

Close-up of playing pieces

Papier (and Clay) Mâché }

CREATE LITTLE WOODLAND CREATURES and mushrooms by covering a clay model with strips of decorative book pages. Embellish them with pens and ink, gouache paints, and colored markers.

Artist: Pam Garrison

✄ **MATERIALS**
book pages (cut or torn into strips)
air-drying modeling clay
PVA glue
glue brush
ink and pen
colored markers
gouache paint and brush
wooden dowel

💬 **CONSIDERATIONS**
Almost any shape can be modeled and wrapped with book pages: animals, flowers, mushrooms, trees, birds, owls, fantastical creatures, monsters—use your imagination.

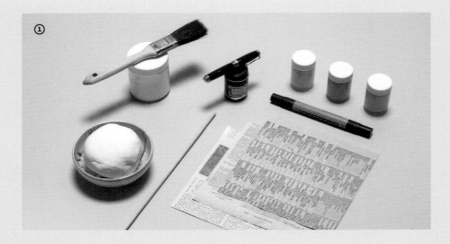

INSTRUCTIONS:

① **STEP ONE: MAKE THE MODEL**
Air-drying modeling clay is lightweight and easy to work with. The overall shape of the model, in this case an owl, can be a little rough, because the strips of paper applied to the surface create texture and visual interest. Wrap a wooden dowel with paper pages and carefully nudge it into the bottom of the model. You'll use this dowel as a handle when wrapping the model and as a stand when displaying the final piece. Allow the modeling clay to air dry before adhering paper strips.

② **STEP TWO: APPLY BOOK PAGES**
Apply strips of book pages to the model using PVA glue and a glue brush. For the first layer, cover the model completely with strips of paper pages. Once the pages are dry, cut additional book pages into specific shapes to complement the model and carefully adhere these onto the surface, to create a decorative layer. Allow the model to dry.

③ **STEP THREE: EMBELLISH**
Use markers, gouache paints, and ink and pen to embellish the model. The little owl in this example was given eyes and decorative elements using black ink and gouache paints.

✸ **TIP:**
Display the finished woodland creatures by placing them into nests or by nudging the wooden dowels into decorative flower pots.

Papier mâché and clay model covered with strips of book pages
and embellished with ink, gouache, and colored markers created
by Pam Garrison

Book Page Wreath

}

CREATE A BEAUTIFUL AND EYE-CATCHING WREATH using dozens of book pages rolled into cone shapes. Choose pages for their color or typographic design, or decorative pages from holiday books.

Artist: Lana Manis

✂ **MATERIALS**
book pages
stapler
white glue
hole punch
wire
cardboard
scissors

🗨 **CONSIDERATIONS**
Work on this project with a crafty child and create the paper cones together. Creating paper cones is easy to learn, requiring just a stapler. The finished wreath is beautiful enough for year-round display.

INSTRUCTIONS:

① STEP ONE: CREATE THE BASE

Cut a 12" (30.5 cm) circle from corrugated cardboard us-ing a compass or by tracing a dinner plate. Wrap one side of the cardboard piece with book pages. You might need more than one page to completely cover the circle. The circle will only be party visible in the finished wreath.

② STEP TWO: CREATE THE CONES

Remove approximately ninety pages from a book that is taller than it is wide, such as a typical hardcover novel. Two sizes of cones are required to assemble the wreath. Create the shorter cones by rolling along the width of the page and the longer cones by rolling along the length of the page. Roll each page into a cone shape and then staple the bottom flat. The staple will be hidden on the finished wreath. You will need approximately sixty long cones and thirty short ones.

③ STEP THREE: ATTACH THE CONES

Attach approximately thirty long cones to the circular cardboard base using white glue. Create an even circle around the entire base. Adhere the remaining large

cones in a circle around the entire base on top of the first layer. Inset this layer toward the center of the base by approximately 3" (7.6 cm); stagger the second layer as shown at right. Finally, layer the short cones on top of the previous layer of long cones. Inset this layer toward the center by 3" (7.6 cm), as well. Allow to dry.

④ STEP FOUR: EMBELLISH AND HANG

Place a decorative element, such as a smaller page-wrapped circle of cardboard or crepe paper with an ex libris book plate, in the center of the wreath. This decorative element will hide the stapled ends of the cones. Finally, punch two holes on the back of the circular base and thread wire through the holes to create a hanging loop.

✺ TIP:

Laminate the book pages with colored paper before roll-ing the cones to create colorful wreaths.

Close-up of book page wreath.

PROJECT NO.

27}

Shaping Books by Hand }

CREATE A DECORATIVE APPLE by trimming and fanning out the pages of a paperback book. Other shapes can be created using templates such as pears, spheres, vases, mushrooms, organic shapes, and more.

Artist: Sheila Daniels

✂ MATERIALS
paperback book
craft knife
chipboard
binder clip
ink and cotton balls
adhesive
stem and leaf

🖢 CONSIDERATIONS
Use a paperback book with at least 100 pages. The more pages in the book, the smoother the shape will appear when fanned open. Use care when working with the utility blade to shape and trim the book pages.

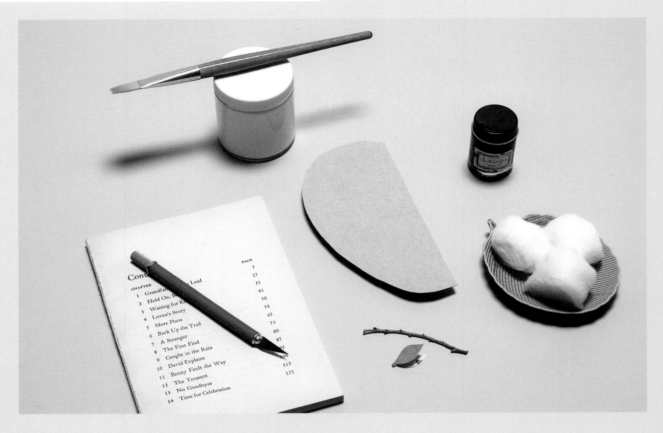

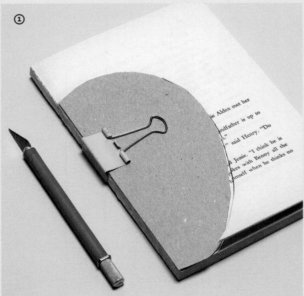

①

②

INSTRUCTIONS:

① **STEP ONE: SHAPE THE BOOK**
Remove the front and back covers from a paperback book and remove any remaining bits of adhesive. Create a template from a piece of chipboard. Attach this template to the book pages with a binder clip and use a craft knife to cut along the template and shape the book. Work slowly and cut through a few page layeres at a time.

② **STEP TWO: COLORING THE EDGES**
Use a cotton ball to spread ink along the edges of the pages and onto the face of each page in a narrow strip, as shown in figure 3. Allow the ink to dry.

③ **STEP THREE: OPENING THE PAGES**
When the ink is dry, fan out the book pages. Attach the first and last pages together with adhesive, or use a few bobby pins to hold the book open. Finish the apple by cutting a paper leaf and attaching it to a natural stem. Insert the stem and leaf into the center of the apple.

✸ **TIPS:**
Creating chipboard templates that are the same height as the book eliminates the need to cut through the spine of the book. Additionally, if the template has a flat bottom, the book will also have a flat bottom and will stand on its own.

Paperback book cut in the shape of an apple and fanned open 360 degrees.

PROJECT NO.

28}

Shaping Books
with Power Tools

DESIGN UNIQUE, THREE-DIMENSIONAL bookish objects using power tools and templates. When fanned out, the books have a smooth edge and a variegated typographic pattern that creates texture and visual interest. The steps for this project describe how to create a book vase.

Artist: Jason Thompson

✂ **MATERIALS**
books
PVA glue
router or jig saw
½" (1.3 cm) medium-density
 fiberboard for templates
guillotine cutter

🗩 **CONSIDERATIONS**
This is an advanced project and requires the use of both power tools and a guillotine cutter. The process creates a beautiful piece of book art suitable for display. Use your imagination and create functional and decorative items such as this flower vase or other bookish shaped objects.

INSTRUCTIONS:

① STEP ONE: TURNING THE BOOK INSIDE OUT

The key to creating a smooth edge on both the inside and outside edges of the vase is to begin with book blocks that have been turned "inside out." Turning the book blocks inside out removes the glue, sewing, and messy spine from the book block and creates clean edges on both the inside and outside edges of the vase.

Begin by removing the covers from any hardcover or paperback book. You'll need additional books of the same size for this step, because the vase requires many book pages. (For example, a vase with a center diameter of 1.25" [3.2 cm] requires a stack of book pages, before fanning them out, approximately 4" [10.2 cm] in depth.) Use a guillotine cutter to slice away a thin strip from the front edge (fore-edge) of the book block to create a clean edge. Glue-up this front edge with several applications of PVA; this will glue the pages together. Once the front edge has dried, use the guillotine cutter once again to slice away the spine. The result is a book block turned inside out with two clean edges.

② STEP TWO: CREATING THE TEMPLATES

The templates used for this project were custom laser cut. They are designed with a computer program and delivered electronically. Although you can find laser-cutting shops locally or through online vendors, you don't need to go through the effort of creating laser-cut templates—they can be created with a tabletop jig saw. The templates need to be created in pairs and should include several bolt holes. The material used for the templates in this example is ½" (1.3 cm) medium-density fiberboard.

③ STEP THREE: CUTTING THE BOOK

Place the inside-out book block between the templates and bolt the templates together. If the bolts are placed close to the router bit guide, the pressure will securely hold the book block in position. Additionally, you can use temporary adhesive, such as double-sided tape, to keep the book block from shifting. Once the block is placed inside the template, use a bearing-guided straight bit and follow the channel of the template to cut through

the book pages, creating book blocks trimmed
to the exact design of the template.

④ **STEP FOUR: FANNING OUT THE BOOK**
Stack the shaped book blocks together and apply
several applications of adhesive to the inside
edges. This step will create one complete stack
ready to be fanned open. Fan them open the full
360 degrees and use PVA to adhere the first and
last pages together. The center of the vase will
not remain circular unless it is held open with
a glass test tube or other circular object. Once
the test tube is placed inside the center, the vase
will stand on its own and the pages will fan out
evenly.

....

✹ **TIP:**
Advanced Tip: Once Step Three is complete
and the book block is trimmed into several
same-sized vase shapes, they will need to be
glued together. I've found that slight shifting of
the book block within the template sometimes
occurs, creating uneven edges on the inside of
the vase. This unevenness isn't noticeable until
the shapes are stacked up and ready to be glued
together. Overcome this issue by carefully lining
up the outside shaped edges and only gluing the
top and bottom (head and tail) portion of the
shaped book blocks. Once the top and bottom
are glued and dry, return to the guillotine cutter
and slice off the uneven back edge. The glue on
the top and bottom will hold the entire piece
together during this step. Apply several layers
of adhesive to the new straight and even back.

Once dry, return the piece again to the guillotine
cutter and carefully cut away the top and bottom
glued edges. The book pages can now be fanned
out 360 degrees. These extra steps add time to
the project, but the result is a perfectly shaped
vase, both inside and out.

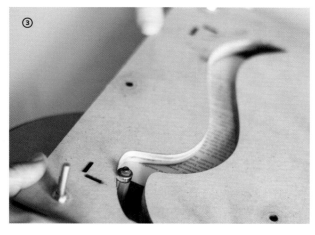

CHAPTER

}

My Echo, My Shadow and Me

A Writer's Notebook

The Music In His Head In Book

Love's Labour's Lost Rings

BETTY PEPPER is a textile and jewelry designer. To find that elusive something that makes an object desirable and "magical," Betty explores different media and techniques in both two and three dimensions. Her work is inspired by stories, memories, things from the past, over-hearings, and misgivings.

A strand of humor runs through Betty's work, which uses word games, hidden messages, and secrets. The work features "grown-up" interests, but they are treated with a childlike attitude. Fabrics—the way they fade, carry scents, and act as memory aids—fascinate Betty, and recycling old garments and fabric has become an important part of her work. The jewelry she creates with this aging fabric seems to have tales of its own to tell, with traces of perfume, old buttons, and thread. Imagine the stories these inanimate objects would tell if they could speak.

Photos: Betty Pepper

Tab/2005. Altered set of encyclopedias, 51″ × 10.25″ × 7.5″
(129.5 × 26 × 19 cm)
Image courtesy of the artist and Packer Schopf Gallery

Webster Two Point Oh/2008. Altered books, 11.5″ × 19″ × 11″
(29 × 48 × 28 cm)
Image courtesy of the artist and Kinz + Tillou Fine Art

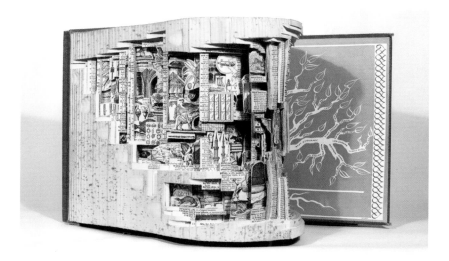

Core 6/2009
Altered book, 11.625″ × 6.75″ × 5″
(29.5 × 17 × 12.5 cm)
Image courtesy of the artist and
Kinz + Tillou Fine Art

BRIAN DETTMER sifts through stacks of old books, boxes of dusty cassette tapes, and piles of obsolete maps to uncover the perfect source and subject for his conceptual explorations and sculptural dissections. Dettmer alters pre-existing materials by selectively removing and manipulating elements as a way to allow new interpretations and ideas to emerge. With the precision of a surgeon, Dettmer uses clamps, scalpels, and tweezers to recontextualize his found objects and reveal hidden meanings. Brian Dettmer has exhibited extensively in galleries and museums throughout North America and Europe.

PLAYING WITH BOOKS

Word Hive. Encaustic, book

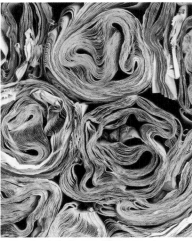

Eccentric Circles/2007. Photograph

Winston's/2004. Photograph

CARA BARER'S photographs are primarily a documentation of a physical evolution. She has changed a common object into sculpture in a state of flux. The way we choose to research and find information is also an evolution. She hopes to raise questions about these changes, the ephemeral and fragile nature in which we now obtain knowledge, and the future of books.

She arrives at some of her images by chance. Others, through experimentation. Without these two elements, her work would not flow easily from one idea to the next.

She realized she owned many books that were no longer of use to her, or for that matter, anyone else. Would she ever need *Windows 95*?

After soaking it in the bathtub for a few hours, it had a new shape and purpose. Half Price Books became a regular haunt, and an abandoned house gave her a set of outdated reference books, complete with mold and neglect. Each book tells her how to begin according to its size, type of paper, and sometimes its contents.

With the discarded books that she has acquired, she is attempting to blur the line between objects, sculpture, and photography. This project has become a journey that continues to evolve.

A final note: No important books have been injured during the making of any of these photographs.

Disasters; Twisted Series; Yellow Pages/2002
Altered phone book, 14″ × 15″ × 5″ (35.5 × 38 × 13 cm)

Fault Lines/2003
Altered atlas, 18″ × 12″ × 1.75″ (46 × 30.5 × 4.5 cm)

Ruffled Collar/2004
Altered book, 8″ × 11″ × 11″ (20 × 28 × 28 cm)

Tract, Ryder University/2003
Fifty romance and mystery novels, 4′ × 8′ × 0.5′
(1.2 × 2.4 × 0.2 m)

Theoretically and physically DOUG BEUBE "excavates" the book, as a phenomenological endeavor, creating hypertexts, as if the text block itself is an archaeological site. When he appropriates books, their words are sometimes readable, their shapes are sometimes recognizable, but in every case they are transformed into objects that are visual and speak volumes. Relinquishing their secrets requires numerous readings. Through the use of various power tools, the text of the book is reconfigured into abstract forms and editorializes the notion of a book into sculpture.

Wild Flowers/2006 Book, glass, wood

Since its invention, paper has been used for communication, both between humans and in an attempt to communicate with the spirit world. SU BLACKWELL employs this delicate, accessible medium and uses irreversible, destructive processes to reflect on the precariousness of the world we inhabit and the fragility of our life, dreams, and ambitions.

It is the delicacy, the slight feeling of claustrophobia, as if these characters, the landscape, have been trapped inside the book all this time and are now suddenly released. A number of the compositions have an urgency about them, the choices made for the cutout people from the illustrations seem to lean toward people on their way somewhere, about to discover something, or perhaps escaping from something. And the landscapes speak of a bleak mystery, a rising, an awareness of the air.

Out Of Narnia/2008 Book, glass, wood, lights

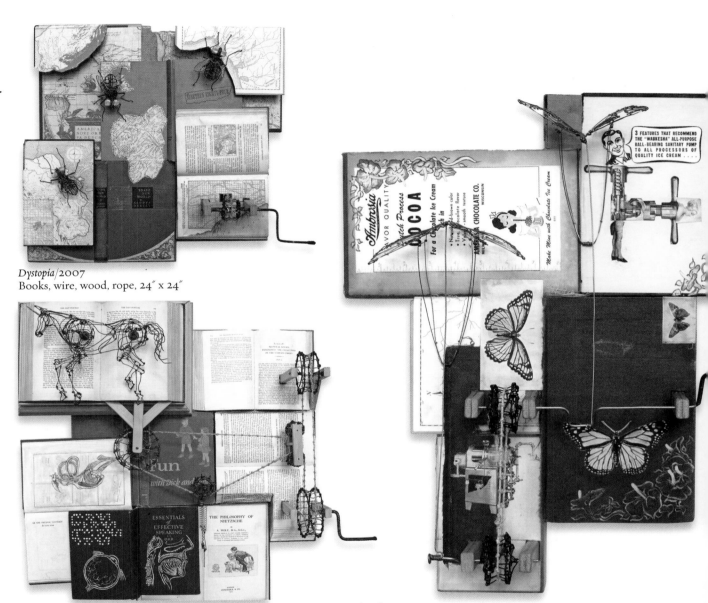

Dystopia/2007
Books, wire, wood, rope, 24″ x 24″

Cream: A Study in Instant Gratification/2007
Books, wire, wood, rope, 20″ x 14″ (51 x 35.5 cm)

Dick and Jane Have a New Game/2007
Books, wire, wood, rope, 30″ x 30″

CASEY CURRAN'S kinetic sculptures rely on the physical link between viewer and art. Studying semiotic relationships as a visual vocabulary, she creates physically moving archetypes and naturally bound forms as a vehicle for various ideas and images. Within her work, associations focusing on literature, philosophy, and nature are often highlighted in these kinetic environments.

Photos: Casey Curran

Eternellement II/2009
Cut and painted sheet music in
acrylic case, 58.5″ × 47″ × 3.5″
(148.5 × 119 × 9 cm)

Classiques/2007
Cut book in bell jar, 17.5″ (44.5 cm) high

Le Mariage Parfait/2007
Description: Cut book in bell jar,
19.5″ × 15.7″ × 8.5″ (49.5 × 40 × 21.5 cm)

GEORGIA RUSSELL slashes, cuts, and dissects printed matter, which she then manipulates and reconstructs into extravagant, ornamental, and sculptural paper-works. The decorative qualities and inherent potential of her found ephemera are fully exploited as she transforms books, music scores, prints, newspapers, maps, and photographs—sometimes with flamboyant color and wild cutting or with a discreet play on the subject or title of her printed matter. Born in 1974 in Scotland, Russell studied fine art at Aberdeen University and later studied printmaking at the Royal College of Art in London. Her work with books began during a Royal College artists' residency in Paris when she was a student—she became fascinated by the bouquiniste stalls by the Seine. She says that old books have always seemed to her like sculptural objects "representing the many hands which have held them and the minds they have passed through," and states that she has always chosen something that "holds within it a sense of its own personal history, an object which has a secret life," and wants to resurrect her fragile materials and give them "a new life and new meaning." There is a simultaneous sense of loss and preservation in each construction; she wants to retain and reclaim the past as much as her techniques attack it.

PLAYING WITH BOOKS

Tectonic II: In the Rockies/2007
Eroded encyclopedia, graphite, wood, 26.25″ × 11.25″ × 8.25″ (66.5 × 28.5 × 21 cm)

Petra
Eroded Encyclopedia Britannica, pigments,
11″ × 8.75″ × 12.5″ (28 × 22 × 32 cm)

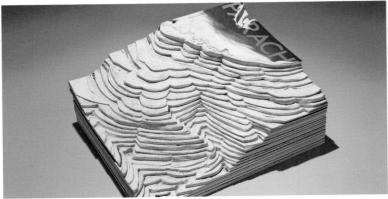

Parachute 1982–2007/2008
Eroded magazines, 12″ × 9.25″ × 6″ (30.5 × 23.5 × 15 cm)

GUY LARAMEE is an interdisciplinary artist who, since 1981, has found his way through such varied and numerous disciplines as stage writing, stage directing, contemporary music writing, musical instrument design and building, singing, video, scenography, sculpture, installation, painting, and literature. He founded the internally acclaimed music ensemble TUYO. He received more than twenty grants and was awarded the Joseph S. Stauffer award for musical composition by the Canada Council for the Arts. He has worked with such prestigious collaborators as Robert Lepage (Québec), Volker Hesse (Zurich), Rachel Rosenthal (Los Angeles), and Larry Tremblay (Montréal). Since 2000, he has worked almost exclusively in the field of visual arts, in which he uses the theme of the erosion of culture(s) as a way to articulate an anthropology of consciousness. His work has been seen and heard across Canada, the United States, Belgium, France, Germany, Switzerland, Japan, and Latin America.

Anthologia (Devotion Series)/2008
Used assembled books, hand-painted and sanded,
burnished inks, bookmarks, archival glue
Photo: Paul Kodama

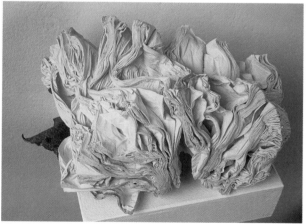

Shrunken Encyclopedia (from Ex Libris)/2000
Petrified book, high-fired book in kiln, 7″ × 15″ × 7″
(18 × 38 × 18 cm)
Photo: Brad Goda

Stack (from Volumes)/2001–2002
Manipulated Books

JACQUELINE RUSH LEE considers herself an experimental artist who works decisively and intuitively between the borders of craft and fine art to create sculptures informed by personal and art historical ideas. She transforms used books into artworks that create new narratives. She is interested in how these objects come with their own histories of use and meaning.

Many of the techniques she employs are informed by both traditional and nontraditional artistic practices. She is interested in mainly using the pure components inherent in the books themselves—inks, covers, pages, book marks, book headbands—and scrambling the formal arrangement of them. She is interested in the fact that the books have been lovingly handled, marked, and cared for by another hand and hopes to enhance these qualities through her finished works.

Holes/2009 (detail)
Altered book, 8″ × 10.5″ × 1.5″ (20 × 26.5 × 4 cm)

Ashes/2008
Altered book, photograph, 10″ × 8″ (25.5 × 20 cm)

Golden River Music Book/2009 (detail)
Vintage book, music box element, 9″ × 5″ × 1.5″ (23 × 13 × 4 cm)

Recently, JENNIFER KHOSHBIN has been working with books as a sculptural material. Although paper is often a delicate form associated with a thin surface, she is finding ways to present its conceptual depth. In addition to cuttings, she often adds fine-line drawings or photo images to re-script the story. Because the encounter with text has now become mostly an onscreen experience, she is tunneling into vintage hardbound texts to explore the dubious future of the book itself, trying to imagine what it might be like for books to undergo a kind of adaptation for survival.

One compositional theme she has not been able to escape or exhaust has to do with the line between rewriting and remembering the past. The nostalgia for childhood experience produces a number of questions: What constitutes "true past?" How do we rewrite our story? How can one recover a worldview free of adult limitations and anxieties? The memory of childhood is often obscured by a fountain of distortions, and when she looks at her own history, much of it is often missed or misunderstood. However certain she is about this fact, she is never really sure how she should feel about it—deluded or emancipated or blind, or just average? Her artwork is a way of shuffling and dealing from this deck of possibilities.

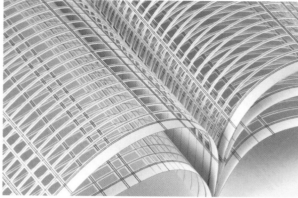

Untitled (M. Sylvia's Book)/2009 (detail)
Hand-cut ledger paper; dimensions variable,
approximately 9″ × 18.5″ × 3″ (23 × 47 × 7.5 cm)

Untitled (U.S. Capitol Building)/2008 (detail)
Hand-cut ledger paper; dimensions variable, approximately
8.5″ × 15″ × 7″ (21.5 × 38 × 18 cm)

Untitled (U.S. Capitol Building)/2008
Description: Hand-cut ledger paper; dimensions variable,
approximately 8.5″ × 15″ × 7″ (21.5 × 38 × 18 cm)

Ledger sheets are traditionally used to record the financial transactions of a business or an individual. These papers host the data necessary for accounting information to be compiled and for analysis in determining profit and loss. They are the material of economics.

In an attempt to understand our need to quantify our transactions, JILL SYLVIA employs this paper. The artist uses a drafting knife to individually remove tens of thousands of boxes from this paper, leaving behind the lattice of the grid intended to separate the boxes. She involves herself in this routine of trying to make time and labor palpable while communicating its loss. She is concerned with the manner in which this material is recontextualized by way of process (and consequent futility) and how the resulting voids suggest "that the methods we employ to arrange our world provide more insight into ourselves than that which we seek to organize."

The skeletal pages drape and accumulate, demarcate the time cost for their creation, and become the buildings for which they have laid the groundwork. Grids are reconstructed using the excised boxes to create a new sense, a new value. The boxes become the units of the picture plane, the medium of color fields.

With each piece, the notion of "value" is called into question—be it the value of our quotidian pursuits, the relative value of labor, or the implicit values of economic advancement.

Reading Chairs/2007. Books, recycled wood, pencils, 5.5″ × 6″ (14 × 15 cm)
Photo: Kim Harrington

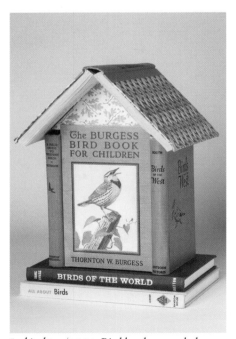

Larkitechture/2009. Bird books, recycled
wood, 14″ × 9″ × 8″ (35.5 × 23 × 20 cm)
Photo: Eric Smith

Mitered Table/2007. Encyclopedias, recycled wood, 20″ × 20″ × 20″
(51 × 51 × 51 cm)
Photo: Kim Harrington

JIM ROSENAU was raised in a house with 5,000 books. He has been making and selling thematic bookshelves from vintage books since 2002. The idea occurred to him years earlier after reading an essay, "Books As Furniture," by Nicholson Baker. Given his background as the son and grandson of publishers, he assumed the reaction, should he make such a thing, would be furious. The work, once underway, proved him wrong. His book furniture has since earned him a wide following with work sold in almost fifty states and countries. The work has been widely published in print and on the Internet. Previously he has been a carpenter, comedy writer (with Charlie Varon), editor, software developer, and planning commissioner; he has also designed and built parade floats.

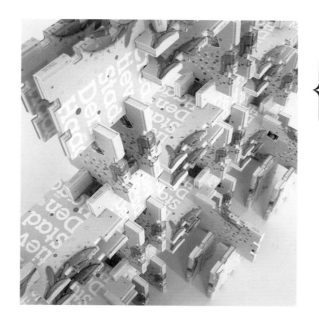

Creative City The Hague/2009
Artists: Trapped In Suburbia, Cuby Gerards, Karin Langeveld,
Debora Schiltmans. Die-cut, printed book

The program Creative City The Hague has been up and running for three years. This publication gives good insight in these results. The book is a building block, and all the books together make a beautiful construction, which symbolizes all the creative people working together making the creative city.

Photos: Robert Verhagen

Phonebook Dress/2009
Phone books, thread

KELLY MURRAY creates a sense of nostalgia by using familiar materials. Whether it is altering a telephone book page or waxing pieces of paper together, she can achieve something new with something old. Simple things inspire her: creating subtle textures and unexpected patterns, giving objects such as old books or a cluster of feathers a second life. *Phonebook Dress* was her initial exploration of the collision of these things and her interest in fashion as art.

Room For Improvement/2009. Papier mâché book pages

Six Dead to Remember/2006
Mixed-media and found-book sculpture, 3.5″ × 3.75″ X 3.75″
(9 × 9.5 × 9.5 cm)

A Little Afraid/2006
Mixed-media and found-book sculpture, 6″ × 4.75″ × 1.25″
(15 × 12 × 3 cm)

Next page: Room For Improvement/2009
Papier mâché book pages

Every time LISA KOKIN takes her craft knife to the tender page of a book, she sees her long-deceased grandfather's face before her. He is not happy. She is committing the Jewish equivalent of a mortal sin, and she feels guilty. So powerful is her drive to rearrange and juxtapose, however, that she willing to risk the wrath of her ancestors to accomplish her mission.

There's something about the silence and intimacy of a book that lets her reveal things about herself that she wouldn't divulge if she were working in another form. Shy by nature, she likes the medium of written word and image and the intimacy between reader and artist it creates. Her definition of "book" is open-ended, a freedom that is in many ways attributable to her lack of book-art training.

Kokin's current series of "reassembled" books is not readable in the traditional sense. She scoops out the contents of the book, remakes it into papier mâché, and then sews or glues the reconstituted contents back into the book. Bits and pieces of the original text float to the surface; the literal meaning is lost. The covers can no longer contain their unruly text, and form defines content.

Twelve Months of Drama for the Average Church/2009
Ink, acrylic, and colored pencil on books, 28″ × 9″ × 6″ (71 × 23 × 15 cm)

When the Animals Rebel (installation)
Commission, Rice University Art Gallery, 16′ × 44′ (5 m × 13.4 m)
Photo: Nash Baker

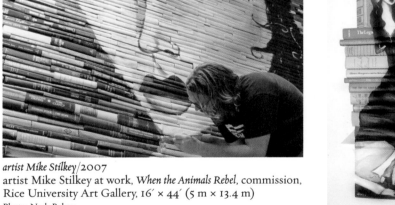

artist Mike Stilkey/2007
artist Mike Stilkey at work, *When the Animals Rebel*, commission, Rice University Art Gallery, 16′ × 44′ (5 m × 13.4 m)
Photo: Nash Baker

A Love Eternal/2009
Ink, acrylic, and colored pencil on books, 29″ × 9″ × 6″ (73.5 × 23 × 15 cm)

Los Angeles native MIKE STILKEY has always been attracted to painting and drawing—not only on vintage paper, record covers, and book pages but on the books themselves. Using a mix of ink, colored pencil, paint, and lacquer, Stilkey depicts a melancholic and at times whimsical cast of characters inhabiting ambiguous spaces and narratives of fantasy and fairy tales. A lingering sense of loss and longing hints at emotional depth and draws the viewer into their introspective thrall with a mixture of capricious poetry, wit, and mystery. His work is reminiscent of Weimar-era German expressionism, and his style has been described by some as capturing features of artists ranging from Edward Gorey to Egon Schiele.

Photos: Mike Stilkey

Nebulous/The Southern Sky Revealed/2009
Stained plywood arch with fifty-six individual folded books,
8.25′ × 4′ × 2″ (2.5 m × 1.2 m × 5 cm)

Bookworm Ensconced/2006
Cut book, torn and sewn paper object with linen thread,
4″ × 8.85″ × 11″ (10 × 22.5 × 28 cm)

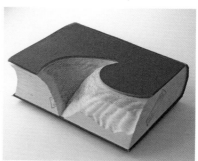

The Blue Wave/2006
Cut English-Sanskrit dictionary,
3.5″ × 11.5″ × 9″ (9 × 29 × 23 cm)

The Kiss/2008
Torn paper and linen thread, 5″ × 4.75″ × 4.75″ (12.5 × 12 × 12 cm)

NICHOLAS JONES is a Melbourne-based sculptor who uses books and printed paper to make works that question the manner in which books are read. Books are capsules, vessels designed to hold information, borne of investigation or of personal expression. These objects are often venerated, held aloft as are amulets, as the source of reasoned knowledge, the fecund field awaiting the harvest. Sequestered away in dusty libraries, spines anticipating the eye of the beholder, these books' tactility remains at arm's length.

The physical act of folding, tearing, and sewing book leaves can be considered iconoclastic (extinguishing the fire of reason, perhaps). Although sometimes revered for their content or historical importance, more often than not, books are discarded as cultural detritus. These transformed books aim to highlight the poetic nature of the book as form. As historical phenomena, books have reflected the evolution of mankind, and although besieged by new technologies, the book remains steadfastly both the solver of the riddle and the creator of the labyrinth.

Flashback/2008
Altered books, dimensions variable

Telling The Truth About History, But Not About The Past/2007
Altered book, empty cover: 5.5″ × 8.25″ (14 × 21 cm),
pieces: 2″ × 2″ (5 × 5 cm)

Flashback/2008
Altered books, dimensions variable

The artist's books that NICOLA DALE makes (part of a wider artistic practice) deal with the themes of originality, authorship, and repetition—not because she thinks everything has already been said but because there is always something to add to the conversation, by way of a little rearrangement to the order of things.

Photos: Nicola Dale

Flashback/2008
Altered books, dimensions variable

Mother/2008
Text from early twentieth-century dictionary, 20″ × 14″ × 2″ (51 × 35.5 × 5 cm)

ELLEN BELL has degrees in illustration and theatre design and a master's degree in fine art. She is a conceptual artist who, in her recent work, has manipulated text and paper ephemera into garment forms that communicate complex messages about language and identity.

The starting point for Ellen Bell's work was the *Woman's Own* and *Woman's Realm* magazines that lay around her mother's house during her childhood. Recipes, fashion suggestions, and romantic serials are what she remembers through her mother. Although there is a mockery in using them because of their obvious superficiality, they also provided a gel and method of conformity for women at that time.

Ten years of theatre design and the making of costumes for others inspired Ellen to make something look like a garment until you get close and realize it can't be worn. Like museum pieces, her fragile tissue-paper clothes work is encased, protected from clumsy human hands. Carefully and expertly sewing them from original patterns, Ellen uses household bits and pieces from the past, such as laundry bills, old pound notes and dollar bills, food labels, recipes, and extracts from old magazines and dictionaries, to weave a deeper meaning into her pieces.

"It is the stuff of ordinary domestic life that interests me—the mundane, the uneventful, the unheroic, the quiet, the routine, the monotonous, and the repetitive," Bell says. "To do this, I remake skirts, petticoats, underwear, corsets, and dresses."

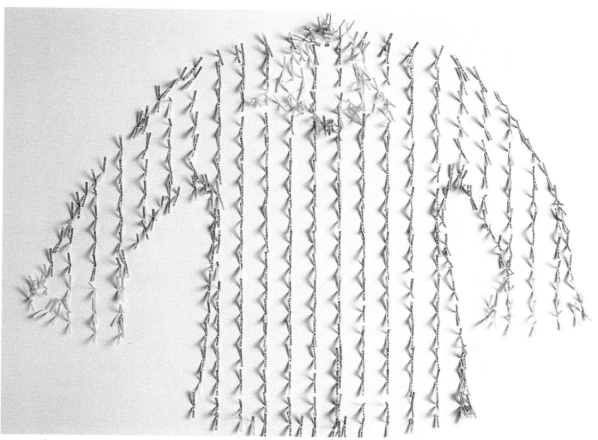

Testament/2005
Text from 1896 edition of Tom Thumb Dictionary, 20″ × 18″ × 2.5″ (51 × 46× 6 cm) Photo: Nigel Cassidy

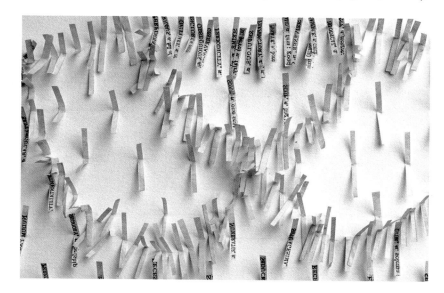

Spelling Testa (2)/2005
Text from early twentieth-century
dictionary, 23″ × 18″ × 2.5″
(58.5 × 46 × 6 cm)

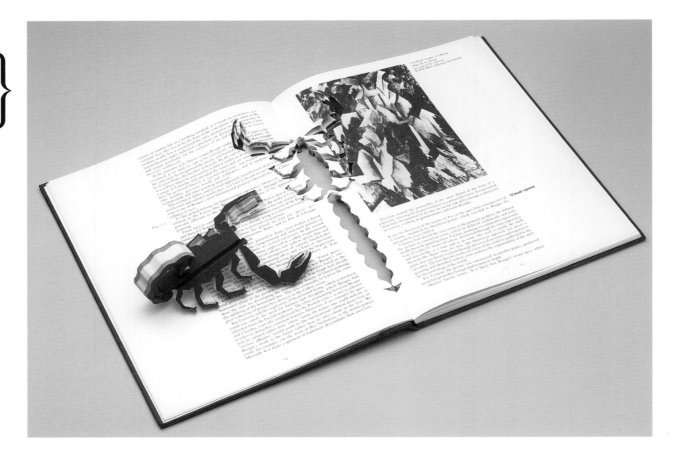

Braque/2006
Altered book, book negative 12.5″ × 9.75″ × 0.75″ (32 × 25 × 1.9 cm), scorpion: 6″ × 4.75″ × 2.75″ (15 × 12 × 7 cm)

Precision vandalized book de/reconstructions and reanimations.

Erotic Art of the Masters/2008
Altered book, 12″ × 8″ × 2″ (30.5 × 20 × 5 cm)

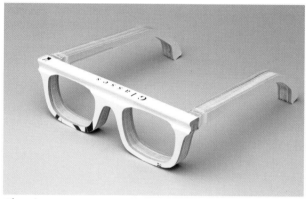

The Medium is the Message/2006
Altered book, book gun: 3″ × 2″ × 0.25″ (7.5 × 5 × 0.5 cm),
book: 4.5″ × 2.75″ × 0.25″ (11 × 7 × 0.5 cm)

Glasses/2009
Altered book, 6″ × 6.5″ × 2″ (15 × 16.5 × 5 cm)

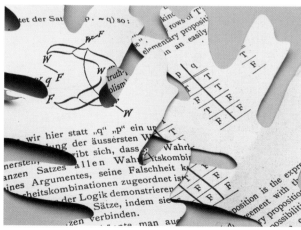

Tractatus/2004
Altered book, book: 8.5″ × 5.75″ × 0.75″ (21.5 × 14.5 × 1.9 cm), leaves: variable

Che
Carved Phonebook

Free Tibet
Carved Phonebook

The One
Carved Phonebook

ALEX QUERAL'S fascination with heads began as an art student. For him, the human head was a natural choice of subject matter because of its inherent expressiveness. He carves the faces out of phone books because he likes the three-dimensional quality that results and because of the unexpected results that occur working in this medium. The three-dimensional quality enhances the feeling of the pieces as an object as opposed to a picture.

In carving and painting a head from a phone directory, he's celebrating the individual lost in the anonymous list of thousands of names that describe the size of the community. In addition, he likes the idea of creating something that is normally discarded every year into an object of longevity.

Photos: Peter Camburn, Projects Gallery

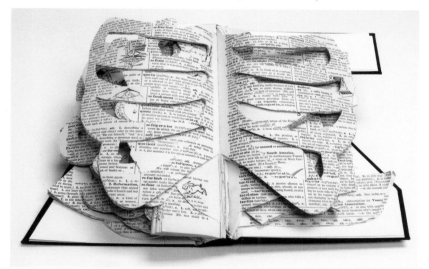

Thirtytwo Paperbacks/2008
Recycled books, wood (poplar), 16′ × 4.5″ × 2″ (40.5 × 11 × 5 cm)

Introvert & Extrovert/2007
Recycled books, wood, 7″ × 5.75″ × 2.25″
(18 × 14.5 × 5.5 cm)

Encyclopedic/2008
Recycled books, linen thread, 3.5″ ×
3.25″ × 25′ (9 cm × 8 cm × 7.6 m)

A to Z/2007
Altered book, 9.25″ × 6.5″ (23.5 × 16.5 cm)

Photos: Susan Porteous

Books and language have been a constant source of inspiration throughout SUSAN PORTEOUS′S artistic practice. She often uses found books as content, both as subject matter and raw material, and her recent explorations have resulted in both sculptural and traditionally bound books. By cutting and rebinding pages into a new form, the relationship between the content of the original book and the resulting form adds an extra layer of meaning and complexity. In adapting traditional binding structures and exaggerating their shape and proportion, the books become more than just containers for information, and their essential physical qualities take on ever more prevalence and meaning. They become sensual objects no longer meant to be read from cover to cover but instead seen as an immediate and cohesive whole.

PLAYING WITH BOOKS

Fathom
Altered book

Lament
Altered book

Swell
Altered book

Teeter
Altered book

Thomas Allen cuts, crimps, creases, and converts the covers of vintage paperbacks into three-dimensional tableaux and photographs them—an idea that feeds his penchant for pop-up books and all other things 3-D. The result is a reimagined look at a product of pop culture whose sales relied more on seductive, eye-popping visuals than literary content, thus proving that you can judge a book by its cover!

Atlas Moth. Hand-cut butterflies from atlas

Beloved Underwing
Hand-cut butterflies from musical pages

Comma, Polygonum C-Album/2009
Hand-cut butterflies from book pages

Tracey uses boxes, paper, thread, entomological pins, and pen and ink to create paper-page butterfly dioramas.

Photos: Tracey Bush

Floor Cluster. Books that have been read are sealed in beeswax and painted

Untitled
Books that have been read are sealed in beeswax and painted

Bound Volumes II
Books that have been read are sealed in beeswax and painted

In art, VERONIKA ANITA TEUBER prefers spiritual and magical things. Since she´s been living in foreign countries, her interest in German Romanticism has grown. Romanticism grows from desire for the eternal. Oppositions, the intelligent light with the tendency to passion and the dark side.

Photos: Veronika Anita Teuber

Artist Directory

Thomas Allen
Coloma, MI
thomasallenonline@gmail.com
www.thomasallenonline.com

Cara Barer
Houston, TX
cara@carabarer.com
www.carabarer.com

Ellen Bell
Bath, UK
ellen.bell@virgin.net

Doug Beube
Brooklyn, NY
dbeube@mindspring.com
www.dougbeube.com

Su Blackwell
London, UK
su@sublackwell.co.uk
www.sublackwell.co.uk

Tracey Bush
Surrey, UK
www.traceybush.com

Nicci Cobb
Houston, TX
reniccicobb@hotmail.com
www.librarianship.etsy.com

Casey Curran
Seattle, WA
caseycurran@mac.com
www.caseycurran.com

Nicola Dale
Manchester, UK
www.axisweb.org/artist/nicoladale

Sheila Daniels
Loda, IL
cheekymagpie@gmail.com
www.cheekymagpie.com

Brian Dettmer
Atlanta, GA
brian@briandettmer.com
www.briandettmer.com

Pam Garrison
Coto de Caza, CA
pamgarrison@gmail.com
www.pamgarrison.typepad.com

Mollie C. Greene
Greenville, SC
molliegreene@gmail.com
www.royalbuffet.etsy.com

Nicholas Jones
Melbourne, Australia
www.bibliopath.org

Jennifer Khoshbin
San Antonio, TX
jennkhosh@yahoo.com
www.jenkhoshbin.com

Lisa Kokin
Richmond, CA
www.lisakokin.com

Guy Laramee
Montréal, Québec, Canada
guylaramee@cooptel.qc.ca
www.galerielacerte.com

Jacqueline Rush Lee
Kailua, HI
phoenix9@hawaii.rr.com
www.jacquelinerushlee.com

Lana Manis
Robbins, TX
lanamanis@gmail.com
www.honeysucklelane.com

Kelly Murray
Indianapolis, IN
kelmurra@iupui.edu

Betty Pepper
Ipswich, Suffolk, UK
betty@bettypepper.co.uk
www.bettypepper.co.uk

Susan Porteous
Denver, CO
sporteous@gmail.com
www.susanporteous.net

Alex Queral
Philadelphia, PA
www.projectsgallery.com

Jim Rosenau
Berkeley, CA
jim@thisintothat.com
www.thisintothat.com

Georgia Russell
London, England
info@englandgallery.com
www.englandgallery.com

Kristin Sollenberger
Wakefield, RI
kristin@myopicbooks.com
www.myopicbooks.com

Ilira Steinman
Pawtucket, RI
ilira@ragandbone.com
www.ragandbone.com

Mike Stilkey
Los Angeles, CA
www.mikestilkey.com

Jill Sylvia
San Francisco, CA
www.jillsylvia.com

Veronika Anita Teuber
New York, NY
vateuber@earthlink.net
www.vateuber.com

Robert The
Kingston, NY
the@bookdust.com
www.bookdust.com

Jason Thompson
Pawtucket, RI
jason@ragandbone.com
www.ragandbone.com

Trapped In Suburbia/Cuby Gerard,
Karin Langeveld, Deborah Schiltmans
The Hague, Netherlands
info@trappedinsuburbia.nl
www.trappedinsuburbia.nl

} About the Author

Jason Thompson is the founder of Rag & Bone Bindery, in Pawtucket, Rhode Island, a bookbinding studio dedicated to creating unique hand-bound books and albums for the gift and stationery industries. He is a self-taught bookbinder and book and paper artist who has been drawn to the solitary and cultural aspects of books since he was a child growing up in urban New England. After walking away from formal schooling at the age of fifteen, he journeyed across the United States on foot from Los Angeles, California, to Washington, D.C., where he kept a journal and discovered a love of journaling and diary keeping. After moving to Providence, Rhode Island, in 1990, he founded the bindery and married and partnered with Rhode Island School of Design graduate Ilira Steinman. Together, in 2004, they renovated a historic mill building as a permanent home for Rag & Bone Bindery, their new family, and their growing book collection. Jason enjoys raising two small children around books and art and hopes to inspire and pass on the love of book making to the next generation.

Acknowledgments

I dedicate this book to my lovely daughter, Faye, who inspires and reminds me every day with her boundless creativity that you can do anything you put your mind to.